Natural Police

Philip Gospage

ISBN: 9798359933087

Briefing

Natural Police

Briefing

In business language, there are hard skills and soft skills. Hard skills refer to the job-related knowledge and abilities that Police officers require to perform their duties. Soft skills on the other hand are personal qualities or interpersonal skills that help officers thrive in the workplace. In order to connect effectively with both offenders and the general public it is necessary to possess and develop what is known as 'People' skills or 'soft' skills.

In my experience, the Police training of the technical skills (hard skills) such as interviewing procedures, officer safety and knowledge of legislation, is excellent and comprehensive. A substantial amount of time is also rightly dedicated to diversity and racial issues. However, little time is set aside for developing the soft skills in individuals that are essential for achieving effective outcomes.

Although these skills are more to do with the general attitude and personality of the individual, they are as important as training officers in the hard skills. There is a school of thought that when it comes to soft skills, **you've either got it or you haven't**. Personally, I disagree with this view because I have witnessed colleagues who have worked hard to develop skills such as active listening and problem solving and have become better officers as a result of doing so.

I was inspired to write about 'soft skills' in policing as a result of encouragement by Jerry H. Ratcliffe. I was privileged to have worked with Jerry at Bow Police Station in London in the 1980's on a neighbourhood policing team in Bow, East London, where I was his Sergeant. He is now a Professor of Criminology at the Temple University in Philadelphia, U.S.A. having been a research advisor to the F.B.I. and the Philadelphia Police commissioner as well as being a published author and podcaster. He works with Police agencies around the world on crime reduction and criminal intelligence strategies. He referred to me in his book titled, **'Reducing crime – a companion for Police leaders'** and compared me to a well-known detective in the HBO series - 'The Wire'. He recognised from working with me that some officers had an uncanny knack of connecting with offenders in a way that they respected, by understanding their needs and motivation. This enabled them to gather intelligence from criminal sources and develop informants. The term **'Natural Police'** was used in the series and it appears to relate to officers who display a combination of intelligence, curiosity, empathy, tenacity and related Policing skills.

A century ago, Chief Constable Wensley of the Criminal Investigation Department of New Scotland yard was aware of the value of 'Natural Police'. He wrote that it was essential to employ detectives who know rogues by direct contact, know their habits, their ways of thought, their motives and above all their friends and associates. In the vast majority of cases information can only be gained in this way, by drinking with them, eating with them and mixing in a variety of circumstances. Wensley was a famous detective of his time, having patrolled the streets of Whitechapel at the time of the Jack the Ripper murders and being involved in Policing the Siege of Sidney Street incident.

It is very flattering that Jerry referred to me in these terms and that I was the first officer he knew who displayed these qualities. I am pleased that he remembered me after all these years and that I may have had some positive input into his future success. Throughout my own career, I have worked with other Police officers who have recognised these qualities in me and have encouraged me to put pen to paper in order to pass my knowledge on. I have also worked with officers who have had similar qualities and who I learnt a lot from. I feel that I have been just an ordinary 'copper' and I was privileged to have worked in the job and learnt my street craft from more experienced constables who were willing to invest time in me.

I reflected on the use of the term 'Natural Police' and I believe it can relate to officers, maybe similar to myself, who have good instincts and have developed their 'soft' skills in their professional capacity. They appear to be dedicated to their role rather than solely being interested in gaining promotion to a higher rank. They do not have to be a detective to display these qualities as was the case with Chief Constable Wensley and his colleagues, but are officers who can connect with the public and criminals alike and who are respected by their peers.

In this book I have chosen what I consider to be the thirty most relevant 'soft' skills which are especially useful in Police work and maybe make some individuals stand out as, 'Natural Police'. I have given a chronological insight into uniformed Police work from my era, by giving examples of each skill area through my experiences in my Police career. I have outlined these experiences in the book by recalling them from my memory and I apologise if any of the specific details are slightly incorrect due to the passage of time between then and now. I have defined each one and provided some basic advice about how to develop them on a personal basis. The 30 short chapters also represent my 30 years of Police service.

I have used pseudonyms to replace the true identity of officers or persons that I have come into contact with during my time in the Police and omitted names where I have been unable to obtain permission from them. This is for reasons of privacy.

At this point I would like to make it clear that although I am a former Police Sergeant, I am not a 'poacher turned gamekeeper' and I have the utmost respect for every Police officer who puts on the uniform and patrols the streets to protect the public. Where I have made criticism of modern Police actions, I have hopefully done so in a way to try and be constructive rather than being negative. We all make mistakes in the course of our work and it is important that we all learn from them for our self-improvement.

At the time of writing, the Police service and specifically the London Metropolitan Police is under heavy scrutiny following some serious cases that have brought the organisation into disrepute. These include the murder of Sarah Everard by a serving officer, allegations of misogyny, racism and sexism at Charing Cross Police Station and two officers who have been jailed for taking and sharing photos of two murdered women at a crime scene. These are disgraceful incidents and have had a hugely detrimental effect on public confidence and the morale of the Police.

Hopefully these incidents are rare and not representative of the Police in general, but steps must be taken to re-evaluate policing priorities to rebuild trust and confidence. I believe that a constructive step in the rebuilding process should be for all officers to take some time to reflect so as to develop and improve their soft skills. Again, this is not a criticism of individual officers but we should all constantly be aware of how our words and actions can impact on people, especially in stressful situations.

Soft skills allow us to build relationships inside and outside of work, to get along with and interact with others, and to work collaboratively in all aspects of teamwork. Successful communication is a real skill and the more we develop it together with other soft skills it can make us more effective in our role as Police officers and motivate us to do better things.

I really hope that you can get something positive from the book and maybe learn from my experiences.

Chapter One

Work Ethic

"Talent is cheaper than table salt. What separates the talented individual from the successful one is a lot of hard work." - Stephen King

Work ethic can be defined as a belief in work as a moral good: a set of values centred on the importance of doing work and reflected especially in a desire or determination to work hard.

Becoming a Police officer is a big decision. For some, it is a natural move or a vocation where their parents or relatives were already part of the organisation. For others, like myself, it was an almost accidental opportunity that came along through necessity. Joining the Police for most people can be a total re-adjustment for their life and you have to be aware that there could be a danger that you could be ostracised from your friends, your community or even your family as they may disagree with your decision or motive for joining.

For me, I started my Police career in the City of Liverpool, in the Merseyside Police in May 1977. I did not fit the image of a traditional Police officer as I was of skinny build, barely 5'10" tall and ten stone dripping wet! However, in my favour, I excelled at sport and they were more interested in me being willing to play for their force cricket team than being an active Policeman. (Sport was a very important activity within Police forces at the time of me joining). So I was in!

After initial training I was posted to 'E' Division of the force. This was an area along the south of Liverpool adjacent to the river Mersey. It covered the districts of Speke, Garston and Toxteth (Liverpool 8). This area was later to become infamous for the inner-city riots in the early 1980's. At this time, each area had its own Police Station and reception for prisoner arrests and during my time with the Merseyside Police I had the opportunity to work at all three places.

The late seventies was a bad economic time for the country, with many industrial disputes and strike action by workers. It was particularly bad for the people of Liverpool, with many big employers in the area closing down and therefore unemployment was rife among local people. The deprivation of the area was very visible and obvious to see.

My role was that of a uniform foot patrol officer, out in all weathers and dealing with any incident that I was summoned to or detected as a result of being constantly on the street. It was a hard and challenging environment on low pay and this led to many of my colleagues to leaving for apparently better opportunities. However, I was motivated, I enjoyed the challenge and freedom of the role and worked hard to put myself forward as much as possible to gain knowledge and experience. It was here that I really developed my street craft from more experienced officers, learning from making my own mistakes and developing a healthy work ethic. I learnt the importance of self-discipline, professionalism, punctuality and time management.

In 1980, after three years in the Merseyside Police, I transferred to the Metropolitan Police in London and was posted to 'K' Division at East Ham Police Station. This area of east London was very different to the inner-city areas of Liverpool that I was used to. There was less deprivation, it had a busy shopping area and a very diverse ethnic community. I was surprised by the lack of front-line officers compared to the Policing demands of the area and the dense population. At the time I was there, East Ham was known as a 'defaulters' station where officers were sent who had minor brushes with the law or who had been subject to disciplinary proceedings under the Police disciplinary code. Generally speaking, these officers were very cynical about Police work and I had to keep self-motivated, work hard, stay focused and try to achieve results. I saw my way out of a negative situation by studying for the Sergeants' promotion examination, improving my knowledge of law and procedures and ultimately getting a transfer to another location.

I achieved my goal by passing this examination in 1982 with flying colours and I was promoted to Limehouse Police Station, which is also in East London. This was the start of a true connection to the London Borough of Tower Hamlets and I went on to serve for 15 years as a Police officer on the Borough and then after retiring from the MPS I went on to complete 10 years as a manager with the Local Authority. I had a real feeling of belonging there as my family had all originated from the area and it was there that I developed what turned out to be my speciality of **'Pro-active community policing'** by building and leading neighbourhood teams.

I was fortunate to witness the immense physical and demographic changes to the area from very working class residential to the birth of a new financial city, with huge structures on the Canary Wharf development under the London Docklands Development Corporation (LDDC).

Ten years later, in 1992, I left Tower Hamlets under somewhat unfortunate circumstances and I spent a couple of years on Havering Borough, mostly based at Rainham Police Station, which is an outpost of the MPS. Rainham presented a different type of Policing problem. It was a mix of commercial premises and mostly privately-owned residential property. Because part of the Rainham area was semi-rural and was under-policed there was a high incidence of commercial burglaries, while the residential area produced more than its fair share of domestic disputes to deal with. While I was there I continued with my passion of Neighbourhood Policing under the sector scheme and encouraged my officers to be involved.

In 1994, I moved to Hackney Borough. I spent 9 years at Hackney, City Road and Stoke Newington Police Stations where I saw an increase in gang culture, violent crime and illegal drug supply. I gradually saw this area change and become more 'gentrified' with many young people moving into Hoxton and Shoreditch, where a vibrant club scene developed. This was a tough period of my service for me and I had to be mature enough to acknowledge my mistakes and to deal with my own vulnerabilities.

In 2002, after 25 years of Police service I returned to Tower Hamlets where I remained until retirement in 2007. I was one of the first Sergeants who was posted to the new Safer Neighbourhood Teams (SNT's) at Shadwell where we attracted considerable media attention. The Shadwell area of the Borough was well known for the high number of disturbance calls, youth disorder and drug dealing in the street. It was a considerable challenge and it was during this time that a well-known journalist called Robert Hardman compared me with the fictional Policeman called George Dixon of Dock Green in a newspaper article titled 'Dixon of Drug Green.' Shadwell was Dixon's fictional Policing beat and I was performing the same role that he was depicted in during the television series.

I was fortunate enough to finish my career as a Sergeant on a high, but in my opinion I worked hard throughout my career and developed my soft skills through experience and academic courses.

Chapter Two

Resilience

"Do not judge me by my success, judge me by how many times I fell down and got back up again." - Nelson Mandela.

Resilience can be defined as the capacity to recover from difficult life events, to understand adversity and demonstrate the ability to bounce back after life's' upset. It enables people to have the strength to cope with emotional loss, depression and stress inside and outside the work experience.

There is psychological, emotional and physical resilience but on a personal level I associate resilience as mental and physical toughness. Although resilience is inner strength it is a skill that can be developed over time especially when dealing with workplace stress. In my opinion resilience is a fundamental soft skill for a Police officer to possess because by the nature of the job it throws up regular challenges and stresses like no other.

When I joined the Merseyside Police, I would describe myself as 'green and naive'. I came from a sporting background and although I had experience of being part of a team, I was unprepared with the challenges of dealing with the public in conflict situations or working closely with people who would probably not be your friends in normal life.

I had been subjected to what I would now call discrimination in previous months before joining the Police. In 1977, a southerner living in the North West of

England was a rarity. It was not uncommon to be subjected to verbal abuse from bigoted individuals who viewed Londoners as the enemy in their midst. On occasions, this was more than banter and I became to some extent normalised to it. I remember applying for a job that required a practical driving test to be accepted. The examiner, who was a Liverpudlian, made it quite clear to me before the test that he didn't like Londoners and mimicked my accent. Despite driving to a good standard, he failed me on the flimsiest of reasons and therefore I was unsuccessful in getting the job. In my opinion, his decision was clearly influenced by prejudice. Nowadays, an applicant would challenge the unfairness, but back in the day this route was not an option and you were expected to take it on the chin and put it down to experience.

I needed to develop my resilience in the Police in my early days in training school. After a one-week induction course at Mather Avenue Police Centre in Liverpool my 'intake class' of 5/77 had to complete an intensive, residential training course at Bruche Police training college in Warrington. At this centre, we were joined by new recruits from other northern Police forces and allocated individual rooms. The rooms were very basic and contained a single bed, a wardrobe, a sink and a desk. Men and women were separated in different blocks. There was a long corridor on each floor of the block with the rooms on either side. There were no locks on the doors and therefore privacy was minimal.

The days were full of classroom exercises, examinations on law and physical training such as boxing, swimming and running. The course itself was physically demanding and the training Sergeants were fair but uncompromising. The environment was similar to a military establishment where the staff were always right and the recruits were treated like underlings. There was little or no compassion shown towards recruits and I soon learnt that the system was set up so that you could never win against a member of staff and that you would be a fool to try.

The evenings were your free time, but in reality you were expected to study in your room and prepare for the next challenging day ahead. Recruits were expected to press their uniforms and polish their boots using a process known as 'bulling'. This involved using spit and polish on your boots so that they became so shiny over time that you could literally see your face in them. If there was any spare time in the evening, recruits could use the bar to buy a drink but they were strongly discouraged to leave the centre and drink in the local pubs. In the 1970's the fashion with most men was to have long hair and the recruits with their short back and sides would have been easily identifiable or targeted as Police recruits by local troublemakers.

Late one night at the start of the course, I was in my room when I heard shouting coming from the corridor. It was a group of Lancashire recruits returning from the pub and quite obviously intoxicated. There was a lot of rivalry and competition between officers from different force areas and officers from the county forces were often jealous of the officers from the busier inner cities that held a lot more excitement. Some Lancashire officers in particular openly despised Merseyside officers and sometimes this resentment turned to aggression. I heard the deep northern voice of one of the group echoing in the quiet corridor. I recognised the voice immediately as coming from a large rotund young man, known to be a bully towards some of the more vulnerable recruits. All of a sudden, the shouting reduced to a whisper outside my door. Seconds later the door burst open and the large man entered accompanied by two of his Lancashire colleagues. They immediately started to rough me up and shout verbal abuse such as 'Cockney wanker'. They took my uniform from the locker, stamped on it on the floor and scuffed up the polish on my work boots. They ran out back to their room laughing leaving me with the task of cleaning my kit all over again late at night. It was essential to be smartly turned out at the 9am parade on the drill square and if you weren't you were likely to be kicked off the course.

I was not the only one to be picked on in this manner by the same group of bullies but there was no point in reporting them. (Not that it ever crossed my mind anyway because the Sergeants would not have taken any action against them.) They treated this kind of behaviour as character building with the attitude - 'if you can't deal with this this here, you'll be no good on the street.' However, some recruits who were treated in this way resigned and left the course. I felt sympathy for them but thought that maybe they were not cut out to be Police officers as they did not show the resilience required for the role.

I reflected on my experience and I set myself a goal to complete the course and to move on to the next phase of training. When you are in a situation like this it is important to think positively, eat and sleep well and be more assertive. Looking back on things I feel that this time was necessary to prepare myself for the challenges and stresses of Police work. Thankfully, I completed the course and was part of the 'passing out parade' on a beautiful sunny day in July.

I fully understand that the behaviour of those recruits should not be tolerated. However, it was a different era and access to counselling or making complaints against fellow officers was not an option. I believe that those 'bullies' actually came to respect me because they didn't break me. I don't know what happened to them in their careers, but it wouldn't surprise me if they came to a 'sticky end' for some random misdemeanour due to their attitude or behaviour.

Chapter three

Stealth

"But if intelligence is our only edge, we must learn to use it better, to sharpen it, to understand its limitations and deficiencies – to use it as cats use stealth, as walking sticks use camouflage, to make it the tool of our survival." - Carl Sagan

The definition of stealth is cautious or surreptitious action or movement.

After I left training school I was posted to the 'E' division area of the Merseyside Police. This area is located on the south side of Liverpool, adjacent to the river Mersey. The division covered several areas or towns including, Speke, Garston, Aigburth, Toxteth and the Dingle. Parts of the division were fairly 'well-to-do' places but the majority were inner city areas that suffered from considerable deprivation mainly due to a lack of Government investment.

I had little local knowledge of the area when I started working there so initially I made it my business to learn and find my way about by using an A-Z street map. These were the days before modern technology and satellite-based navigation systems. First of all, I learnt the main streets that criss-crossed each other and gradually I began to familiarise myself with the side streets and alleyways (known as jiggers). It is essential to develop a good knowledge of your surroundings and the geography of the area such as alleyways and cul-de-sacs. I found that it was especially important to know your exact location at all times whilst on patrol, in case of an unexpected incident arising and that you may need urgent assistance from colleagues.

My first Police posting was at Speke Police Station. It was a reasonably modern building at the time I was there and was probably built at the same time as the remainder of the infrastructure that was developed post second world war. The main focus of Speke was the Parade that contained shops in a pedestrian area. There was a fire Station at one end with the Police Station at the other end and a pub, called the Noah's Ark that served customers who resided in the nearby tenement flats. The majority of the housing stock was managed by the Liverpool Corporation and were various states of disrepair. The remainder of the Speke development was of a similar condition but some residents did try and keep their properties tidy and well cared for. Others unfortunately, were not of a similar mindset and had abandoned cars and rubbish festering in their front gardens. Liverpool Airport (now John Lennon airport) is situated to the west side of Speke and there were several large commercial employers nearby including Ford Halewood Motor company, Metal Box and British Leyland factory. At the time of my arrival at Speke, several of these large factories closed down due to the economic situation leaving many of the Speke residents unemployed with little hope of getting another job. It was not unusual to see grown men and women pushing old prams and hand-drawn carts in the street in search of scrap metal and other discarded goods to sell on for a few pounds. It goes without saying, that there was an increase in petty crime driven mainly by desperation and idleness.

I noticed that everything in the Police was done on a small budget in those days. There weren't any modern computers, mobile phones, fast Police cars and everything was supplied through the Liverpool Corporation (the Local Authority) who were virtually bankrupt. The Police wages were very low, but maybe surprisingly, I found that the moral amongst officers was high. The response teams were small in number but very welcoming, almost like a family. Similar to training school, the Sergeants were fair but uncompromising and distant, senior ranks were rarely seen. Quite a few of the older officers had gone through a period of national service and therefore discipline was rigid and 'saluting' an officer of the rank of Inspector or above was still mandatory.

Team shifts were 7am to 3pm early turn, 3pm to 11pm late turn and 11pm to 7am night duty. If you were 'young' in service you would be posted by a Sergeant to patrol a foot beat on your own and the senior constables would patrol in a car. For the first four weeks on division I patrolled with an experienced constable (or tutor constable) called Dave. He had been in the Police for about 10 years, he was of stocky build and I remember that his uniform had a 'worn' look. This gave me confidence that he 'knew his way around the block' and he could look after himself. We patrolled in an old white Leyland Mini car that appeared to be held together by various bits of D.I.Y. material and Dave made the time on duty fun, by his cheerful and positive manner. My first arrest was of a drunk man who had been detained by an old Sergeant in

Garston. It was a very dark, wet night and on our arrival at the scene the Sergeant was holding his push bike in one hand and one of the arms of the intoxicated man in the other hand. It was a scene reminiscent of the film 'The Blue Lamp'. In those days it was quite usual for more experienced officers to hand over detained persons for routine offences to probationary constables like myself. The primary reason was that probationers needed to show that they had made arrests for a variety of offences and had dealt with other incidents such as domestic disputes, traffic accidents and sudden deaths. The probationer was expected to record all details and produce the record of work to the Sergeant periodically by means of regular reviews throughout the first 2 years of service. A probationer's service could be dispensed with at any time through the first 2 years and there was an expectation for officers to be busy and work without complaining. I learnt a lot from Dave and the other officers and adopted some of the techniques and tactics that they used to hunt down and detect offenders.

The emphasis was very much on patrolling on foot to prevent and detect crime. During the daytime officers were instructed to patrol in uniform and be visible by walking on the pavement near the road in full view of the public. At night time the brief was to patrol in a more concealed manner by keeping close to the building line, checking vulnerable premises for break ins. Therefore, patrolling at night was very different to daylight hours.

The Division did not have much in the way of a nighttime economy and after the public houses closed the streets went quiet and were almost devoid of traffic and pedestrians. Even with the absence of street activity it was still the Sergeants expectation that officers would be busy and productive. I would often hear the words from senior officers and experienced constables, "You don't catch criminals in the Police Station." Meaning that your time on duty should be spent patrolling out on your beat. In those days drinking tea in the Police Station, except for allocated refreshment time, was strongly discouraged. This advice was useful and made patrolling officers become more familiar with their beats and they often found tea stops with friendly residents, shopkeepers and security points. Officers also took the opportunity to call into licensed premises to see who was frequenting them and maybe discretely drink a pint or two of beer with the licensee.

To obtain results during these quiet times required a lucky stop of a stolen car or to patrol by stealth. This would often involve spotting an individual loitering without purpose and keeping careful observation of their movements and suspicious behaviour by concealing yourself in the best possible way without the suspect seeing you. It was a 'cat and mouse' approach, and I had several good arrests by using this tactic. It involved me removing my beat helmet, turning down my personal radio so it could not be heard, remaining quiet and blending in with the environment by hiding behind parked cars and street furniture. I used to catch suspects 'red-handed' burgling houses, schools and commercial premises using this method and walking the prisoner back to the charge room much to the surprise and admiration of the Sergeant on duty.

In one such case, I spotted a male loitering late at night, in an alleyway just off Smithdown Road, who then hopped over a wall at the back of a terraced house. I kept observation on him and saw him enter an upstairs open window of the house by climbing on to a building extension at the rear. It was quite obvious that he was entering without authority and with criminal intent. In this situation the anticipation is huge. You notice a physical change in your body when waiting for the suspect to emerge, with your heart pumping quickly and shallow breathing but you must remain as calm as possible. Within a minute or two he came out of the window holding an electrical item in one hand and I caught him as he came back over the wall into the alleyway and placed him under arrest for burglary. He was so shocked that he did not put up any resistance. This shows the benefits of using stealth when patrolling and that foot patrols are useful and beneficial even in modern day Policing.

Hunting suspects of crime is similar to animals hunting their prey in the wild. Not every hunt is successful and results in a meal but stealth is an important skill to develop and requires patience and determination.

Chapter four

Enthusiasm

"Nothing is so contagious as enthusiasm." - *Samuel Taylor Coleridge*

A definition of enthusiasm is intense and eager enjoyment, interest or approval.

It's said that Police work is 95% boredom and 5% extreme excitement. It stands to reason that a Police officer must have a positive attitude and show enthusiasm for the job. During my probationary period of the first two years of service I had to demonstrate to supervising officers that I was competent to do the job and work effectively with the minimum of supervision. You never stop learning and every situation that you deal with is different and usually complex in nature. Every month or so probationary constables had to attend a full day of continuation training. These sessions were run by local Sergeants who focussed on a specific subject for the day. These subjects included, theft, deception, offences against the person, road traffic law and firearms. The sessions were usually interesting and generated much discussion amongst students. Officers were made aware of new legislation and the more obscure offences. It gave me confidence to go out on the streets and put theory into practice. The emphasis with training was to develop a 'can do' attitude with a view to detecting crime and bringing offenders to book.

I remember after one of these training days I went out on my beat on night duty, checking commercial yards and premises for unsupervised loose guard dogs. There had been new legislation passed under the Guard Dog Act that made uncontrolled guard dogs an offence. I gathered evidence in my notebook on one premises where I saw a large German shepherd dog roaming in the yard, untethered and barking aggressively. There was no one working at the premises at the time so I had to return during an early turn to report the person responsible for the dog for the offence. It demonstrated to the Sergeant that I was not only had knowledge of the law but had the initiative and enthusiasm to follow the case through and take action.

It was also important to demonstrate a positive attitude to Sergeants and colleagues and the willingness to volunteer for any task, even if it was just routine. In my first two years I dealt with numerous road traffic collisions, domestic disputes, reports of crime and several sudden deaths. Serving summonses on people and executing arrest warrants were also routine for a foot beat officer.

Before going out on patrol I used to allocate time to keep up to date with crime trends and daily intelligence reports and then set myself a personal goal for the day. It could be as simple as patrolling a particular location or residential block that I hadn't yet patrolled. The important thing was that I had purpose. I was expected to turn up about 15 minutes before the start of duty to prepare for patrol and of course it was in my own time. However, I remember a saying from an old Sergeant of mine - 'if you're on time, you're late!' It meant that you were expected to put a bit of your own time in, otherwise you were not fully prepared to go out on patrol when directed. These words of advice stayed with me all of my service.

If possible, I would work with an officer who had a positive attitude (although patrolling in pairs was often discouraged by the Sergeants). On one particularly busy day on a late turn I walked out of the Police Station in Toxteth, to go to my beat (18 beat) along Admiral Street in the direction of the Dingle. The Dingle is a very working-class area, mostly comprising of terraced housing. It is best known as being a location for filming BBC programmes including 'Bread' and 'The Boys from the Blackstuff'. I walked out with a more senior officer called Billy who had a similar positive approach to the job as I did. He was on way to patrol the adjoining beat to mine and we walked together on way to our beats. We had literally walked 100 yards from the Police Station when we heard loud banging noise coming from the inside of a derelict shop that was insecure. We entered and found a man upstairs covered in dirt and dust holding a hammer and chisel. He was removing the metal water pipes for scrap without permission and after a short interrogation we arrested him on suspicion of burglary. We walked him back to the Police Station where we took him into the charge room, much to the surprise of the Sergeant who had just briefed us and sent us out only ten minutes before.

We interviewed the prisoner and he made a full and frank admission to the offence. We duly charged him and bailed him to attend magistrates' court.

We took our refreshments and on completion of them we were summoned over the radio to speak to the

Sergeant. I immediately thought that we were about to be reprimanded for patrolling together when we made the arrest earlier in the day, even though all we had done was to walk out in the direction of our beats. However, it transpired that he was impressed with our enthusiastic work and he 'rewarded' us by assigning both of us to an urgent call to assist the ambulance service who had found an elderly woman collapsed inside her home. There were no Police cars available to attend the scene and we ran the half a mile or so through the streets to the residential address near Lodge Lane in Toxteth.

On arrival, we saw an ambulance parked outside a slightly run-down Victorian house. The front door of the house was wide open. Inside the house, the ambulance men told us that they had been called to the address where they found the elderly lady apparently dead on the floor of her front room and they felt that the death may be suspicious. I saw that the lady was indeed prostrate on the floor and lifeless. To my surprise there was another woman in the room with her and two small children sitting on the old settee eating chocolate bars and staring at the body as if it was a perfectly normal event. The children were wearing outdoor clothes and the woman, who spoke with an Irish accent, was heavily intoxicated. She tried to explain that the elderly woman had just collapsed suddenly, but we were puzzled about her presence in the house and her relationship to the deceased. It seemed to be a bizarre situation. As Billy was the senior constable, he led the questioning and he was not happy with her account. He immediately called for a C.I.D. officer to attend as he believed that a serious crime had been committed.

20

We detained the woman until he arrived on scene. The C.I.D. officer calmly but firmly interrogated the woman before telling her that she was under arrest for murder. She admitted that she had entered the house by deception with her two children and she 'accidentally' strangled the deceased while asking her for money. The detective gave instructions for us to preserve the scene of crime and to make arrangements for the two small children to be taken into care of the Social Services. We remained at the scene until the end of the shift until the body was removed and a night duty officer arrived to take over the security. The officer actually arrived at about 20 minutes after the end of our duty which was not unusual with handovers of a crime scene.

We left the house into the darkness of the night where a night duty officer was waiting in a battered white Mini Police car with its engine running in order to take us back to the Police Station. The driver, who I knew as Pete, was frantically beckoning us to get in the car and hurry up. As we jumped in he said just two words. "Car chase."

Pete was an experienced officer and we knew that his hobby away from the Police was rally driving in his spare time. Pursuits after stolen cars was a regular occurrence in Toxteth and the local youths (also known as 'Bucks') enjoyed taunting the Police by stealing high powered cars and driving them recklessly around the local streets. They knew that the Police Mini cars were really no match for top of the range high-powered modern cars and the suspect drivers were usually only captured if they made a driving error due to their inexperience and crashed. Suddenly the radio crackled, "Tiber Street, Tiber Street." The pursuing

Police driver was shouting the location of the suspect car and it was coming our way. As the suspected stolen car passed us Pete sped off and joined the two Police cars that were following it. For Billy and I, we were now at work in our own time but returning to the Police Station was not a consideration. We were both enthusiastic officers and wanted to see the job through.

We were then subjected to a terrifying 'white knuckle ride' as the driver of the stolen car tried to shake off the pursuing Police cars through the back streets of Toxteth. Pete was a skilled driver and I remember the screeching wheels, the smell of rubber from the tyres and the loud revving of the car engine. As passengers, we were holding on for dear life and swaying around with the 'G' forces. Then our suspect pulled onto Princes Road, which was a long straight open carriageway. With his high-powered engine he was able to accelerate away from us. The stolen car eventually came to rest by crashing into the front of a house in Upper Parliament Street. The chase attracted a lot of attention and many youngsters had come out onto the street, cheering and encouraging the driver of the car. He ran off, made good his escape and was not detected.

Pete calmly drove us back to the Police Station and dropped us off.

The result of our toils that day were that the man who we found removing water pipes for scrap was given a fine at Magistrates Court for being found on enclosed premises for an unlawful purpose. (Under the Vagrancy Act 1824). The woman who we found in the house and was arrested for murder was charged and later pleaded guilty to manslaughter. She was sent to prison for four years.

As a footnote, a few months later I re-arrested this woman when I found her loitering in an alleyway one rainy, night duty after she had 'escaped' from an open prison by walking out unchallenged!

A week or so later, my reporting Sergeant gave me a review and agreed that I was suitable to be confirmed as a Constable on a permanent basis. I continued to work hard at my role and before leaving Merseyside for the Metropolitan Police they awarded me a three-week driving course. I really enjoyed my time on 'E' division, and I learnt so much about pro-active Policing from other officers, who always supported me. I still feel a connection to the city after all these years.

Chapter five

Self-motivation

"Success is not final, failure is not fatal: It is the courage to continue that counts." - Winston Churchill.

A definition of self-motivation is being driven by one's own desires and ambitions.

Being posted to East Ham Police Station on my transfer to the Metropolitan Police was a different proposition to where I worked before in Liverpool. East Ham was part of 'K' division in the Met. It was a division that stretched from West Ham in the west to Upminster in the east. East Ham had been a fairly 'well-to-do' area around the war years and had been the birthplace of Dame Vera Lynn. Since those days the area had become more diverse with many south Asian families taking up residence, primarily because the area had reasonably cheap housing stock. The High Street and Barking Road were busy shopping areas with West Ham United Football ground situated in Green Street. To the south there was North Woolwich, an area that had its own Police Station. This used to be a very busy area when the Royal docks were operating but since their closure it had become something of a wasteland. Plaistow was part of the sub-division which covered Canning Town and had the reputation of being a much busier area for Police.

There was a slightly fraught relationship between the officers from East Ham and Plaistow because of the perceived 'gung-ho' attitude of the Plaistow officers compared to the more 'laid back' approach of the East Ham staff. I was posted to a team that had a reputation of being lethargic or even lazy. Some of the officers were known as 'defaulters' - in other words officers who had minor brushes with the law or who had been committed a misdemeanour against the Police discipline code. One officer on my team had been sent there following a physical disagreement with a senior officer, two had serious alcohol issues and another openly boasted that he had not written in his notebook for over four years. (Meaning he had avoided doing any meaningful Police work). They were generally very cynical about Police work and suspicious about anyone who showed enthusiasm for the job. Being a newcomer to the team I decided to work with them and attempt to build a good rapport. I came to realise that they were decent and honest people who had experienced either clashes of personality with other work colleagues or had complex problems in their personal lives. Although most of them had little enthusiasm for routine work they would always support me if I required assistance on the 'hurry up'.

I found that I needed to motivate myself by taking responsibility and ownership, learning new skills and setting myself realistic goals.

There was a variety of work available at East Ham, including dealing with shoplifters, performing duties at football matches on match days and hunting for suspects on night duty. I was always busy, making arrests for offences of burglary, theft, public order offences, taking and driving away and drunk driving. I was rewarded for my self-motivation when I was given an advanced driving course at Hendon Training Centre that then allowed me to drive the area or 'wireless' car. This car was always the first to receive emergency 999 calls and took the lead in vehicle pursuits. Passing the course enabled me to have a new skill and the opportunity to work with other officers.

One night duty I was patrolling in a marked Police car on my own when I saw a red pick-up lorry being driven at high speed towards me. It did not initially arouse any suspicion but it failed to give way to me by pulling out in front of a parked car in my path. I could have just ignored it and put it down to a case of bad judgement but being a pro-active Police officer and a self-motivated person I turned the Police car round and set off in pursuit. By the time that I had manoeuvred the car, the pick-up was out of sight, but I had made a mental note of the vehicle registration number and I had observed the driver who was alone in the cab of the lorry. I sped off after it and to my surprise, as I drove around the corner, I saw the pick-up with its brake lights on and the driver jumping out. He ran around the front of the vehicle and into the garden of a house that was hosting a house party. The driver disappeared through the open door of the house as I pulled up behind the lorry. I jumped out of the Police car but thinking on my feet, I realised that chasing a man into a house that was full of people, who probably knew him, was a risky thing to do. I wondered why the driver had run off and everything pointed to him to be guilty of dishonest act. I looked on the back of the pick-up lorry and saw that it was carrying a huge cable drum (like a huge cotton reel) with thick industrial cable wrapped round it. I concluded that the driver must have stolen it from a nearby construction site and realised that the cable itself would have been worth a small fortune in scrap metal value.

I decided to call for the assistance of other officers so that I could conduct a search of the area. Pending their arrival at the scene I conducted a check on the Police National Computer to find out who the registered keeper of the vehicle. Information came back that the lorry was registered to a Robert Bunson. Within a couple of minutes some other Police officers arrived on the scene and I was explaining what I had seen to them when a man appeared from the rear of the house party shouting, "That's my truck, who stole it." I immediately recognised him as the driver who had run away a few minutes earlier.

He had changed his top but he had a hostile approach and he was sweating from his exertions. I confronted him and he became aggressive and defensive. I made a decision to arrest him on suspicion of theft of the cable drum and took him to the Police Station where he was later charged.

Bunson elected trial by jury at Snaresbrook Crown Court, framing his defence around the lack of identification evidence against him. However, despite me only having only a fleeting glimpse of him driving on the night of the incident, the jury were satisfied from my evidence that he had committed the offence and found him guilty of theft.

This was a challenging time, but I remained optimistic about the future and ensured that even if I had a setback I would keep on working and see every task through to the end.

Chapter six

Learning effectively

"Any fool can know. The point is to understand." - Albert Einstein

Learning effectively is the holistic process by which students engage in a high-quality learning experience.

Police work involves a constantly changing environment and no two incidents that an officer may deal with are the same. Continuous learning helps to adapt to unexpected changes and provides you with the essential knowledge to do the job well. By learning you will keep improving and opens your mind to changes in your attitude. It can also give us a feel of accomplishment and in turn boost our confidence to undertake challenges. This means that you could become more competent in your present role, take on more responsibility or even provide you with an opportunity for promotion.

I had already studied for and passed the constable to sergeant promotion examination in Merseyside with flying colours but unfortunately the qualification was not recognised in the MPS as they had a different type of examination to the other force areas. I had a thirst for knowledge and I was keen to learn more about the MPS procedures. I enrolled on the promotion course that was scheduled to last about 6 months with the classes being held at East Ham Police Station. It was facilitated by experienced Sergeants and Inspectors. During the training sessions it was essential to actively listen and make your own notes. The lessons also gave us the advantage of being able to ask questions if we were unsure about a point and also talk to other students to compare our progress. We had to organise ourselves with the learning material and devise our own study plans. We were provided with two huge binders that contained the General Orders and regulations for the Metropolitan Police. They were referred to as 'G.O.' and the contents outlined formal procedures similar to a 'how-to-do-it' guide. There were six parts to the contents.

1. Administration
2. Crime, prisoners, courts, process etc.
3. Traffic, public transport etc.
4. Technical services,
5. Other Police duties.
6. Finance and supplies.

These orders and procedures had been in place for many years and although parts of them were regularly updated, other parts were clearly out of step with the Police work of the day. However, to be successful in the examination, students were expected to learn the procedures by memorising important sections in parrot fashion. There were over 100 sections to learn and were referred to as either 'A' reports or Star reports. An 'A' report could be learnt by summarising or 'précising' the salient points but a star report had to be learnt, word for word.

An example of a star report is as follows:-

"The primary object of an efficient police force is the prevention of crime: The next that of detection and punishment of offenders if crime is committed. To these ends all the efforts of the police must be directed. The protection of life and property, the preservation of public tranquillity, and the absence of crime, will alone prove whether those efforts have been successful and whether the objectives for which the police were appointed have been attained."

This statement was originated by Sir Richard Mayne in 1829. He was the first Commissioner of the Metropolis and this simple statement still holds good today. Although some students were critical of the training methods, I can still remember those reports today, nearly 40 years later.

My study routine was to dedicate two hours every day at home to memorise these reports, read law books such as Butterworth's Police Law and answer hypothetical questions about the application of the law from a magazine called 'Police Review'. (This magazine is no longer published). I used to work upstairs, away from distractions such as noise from the television and children.

Due to the nature of the studying, the wording of the reports were constantly going round in my head and this enabled me to commit them to memory and put them into practice in the real world.

Of course, being an active front-line officer who was working shifts meant that there was no time allocated for study at work as the expectation was that all studying would be done in your own time. This was slightly unfair to front-line officers as colleagues working in office roles were often allowed study time by their supervisors. I saw the course through to the end, keeping to my study plan, despite having to work through often tiring and stressful shifts such as the Brixton riots in 1981, which spilled out into other parts of London and throughout the country. There were some advantages though, because the Sergeants would often give you more responsibility in the charge room, allowing you to book in prisoners and to complete complicated legal papers for Crown Court (known as 'soup' reports). However, I always believed that the majority of the time this work was delegated for their own convenience, in order that they could have an easier duty.

On the day I took the examination, I was so well prepared that I almost knew I had passed when I completed the two papers. Within a couple of months, I received the news that I had been successful and it would only be a short time be a supervisor and leader.

Chapter seven

Decision making and critical thinking

"You can't make decisions based on fear and the possibility of what might happen." - Michelle Obama

Critical thinking is the practice of methodically gathering, analysing and evaluating information. While decision making is the process that leads to actionable conclusions.

Critical thinking defines whether the choice is sound. People make decisions in their life routinely, whether it be a simple choice of having either tea or coffee in the morning or huge ones such as whether to buy a particular house or property.

Decision making in the course of Police work is usually complex, often based on incomplete information or even in circumstances where someone is deliberately trying to mislead. Because officers are dealing with people who often have messy and chaotic lives, it's hardly surprising that some decisions do not achieve the best outcomes. Over the years, the Police service has recognised this and have adopted a framework to assist officers with the decision-making process. They have devised a model that is consistent with the principles and standards of behaviour set out in the code. There are six key elements:-

1. Code of ethics
2. Gather intelligence and information
3. Assess threat and risk and develop a working strategy
4. Consider powers and policy

5. Identify options and contingency

6. Take action and review what happened

Probably the biggest decision that I made in my early years as a Police officer was to undertake the Sergeants promotion examination. I felt that after 5 years on the street I had the necessary experience, dealing with arrests, working on central London aid, policing football matches and dealing with a variety of routine incidents. I had also passed the advanced driving course that permitted me to drive high powered Police cars and respond to Police pursuits and 999 calls. But being a Sergeant was a different kind of challenge. Yes, I was making decisions on the street as a constable but I was basically looking after myself and I had not needed to concern myself with man management.

On my promotion in May 1982, I was posted to Limehouse Police Station in Tower Hamlets Borough. Limehouse was on the same sub-division as Bow and was about one mile from the city of London. At the time, the area was a run down, deprived, dockland area but there were plans to develop the derelict docks and warehouses into a new financial hub.

Early in the 20th century the Limehouse causeway area was populated by the Chinese community and when I arrived there were still several traditional Chinese restaurants serving simple but seemingly exotic food.

Tower Hamlets has always been a melting pot for newly settled immigrants stretching back to the days of the French Huguenots who lived in and around Brick Lane and worked in the clothing and silk trade. The Jewish community later settled in Whitechapel and they were followed by the 'Windrush' generation of West Indians. Latterly, the Bangladeshi community settled in the E1 area. The Borough is rich in social and political history and has always attracted media attention.

There were two other Sergeants on my team. One was relatively inexperienced and the other was much older in service and well respected by the constables. Subconsciously, I tried to emulate him and for the short time that we worked together I learnt a lot from him. For the first year my role was to be the Station officer at either Limehouse or alternatively Bow Police Stations, which meant that I spent most of my time on inside duties, only occasionally patrolling with constables on the street.

Prior to the introduction of the Police and Criminal Evidence Act, the Station officer was responsible for the front office, the reception, detention and welfare of prisoners and many other administrative duties. These included supervision of the duty state, recording incidents in the Occurrence book, checking the bail book 41 and the security of the Firearms cabinet. Basically, the Station officer was responsible for everything that happened in the Police Station building.

It was a challenging time and I made mistakes, but I realised that it is important to learn from the experiences. I soon realised that although Constables had a lot of initiative in those days, they would come to you with their own problems and questions that were very often complex in nature. Sometimes, I had to look for advice from a more experienced Sergeant so that I did not mislead them with incorrect information. I also learnt that there were some officers who on occasions, did not like the answer to a question that they asked. They would then go to another Sergeant with the same enquiry, in the hope of a more favourable outcome. This behaviour was not acceptable and if I found them out I would challenge them or at the very least remember the incident for a future date.

The detention of prisoners was very much a different process back then, with few legal guidelines or risk assessments in respect of the detainees. The instructions for a person's detention were laid out in general orders and the investigation of offences were conducted according to Judges rules. This was a process of 'stated cases' and historic practices that had been tested by the Courts. There was a lot of 'flexibility' within these practices and there were few formal procedures when conducting interviews as this was before the introduction of modern technology used to tape or video questioning of suspects.

As a young Sergeant, I had to develop a firm attitude to constables but still be approachable. There were many vulnerable prisoners brought in the charge room, who had serious problems such as severe alcoholism, mental health and physical disabilities. It was a conveyor belt of humanity and the expectation was to detain them and only in very serious cases would they be transferred to hospital for medical treatment. It was possible to call for a 'Divisional Surgeon' to attend who would treat a prisoner for illness or injury and certify that they were fit to be detained. 'Down and out' drunks were held in a large cell or 'drunk tank' together and it was not unusual for other prisoners to be detained two or three to a cell.

I can't remember ever refusing to accept a prisoner and I'm sure that if I had done so the duty Inspector would have questioned my reasoning. The decisions about risk that we had to make were complex and you often had to rely on your instincts. It was essential to take everything into consideration but not try to overthink things. I remember asking the old Sergeant on the team for advice and feedback about managing the prisoners in the cells in my early days there. He told me "Don't let them die on you and don't let them escape. Anything else you do is a bonus." It was simple but excellent advice and something that I always remembered throughout my service. Of course, the last thing any officer in charge would want is a death in the cells as not only would it be a tragedy in itself, but there could be massive repercussions in the form of disciplinary proceedings or even legal action being taken against you.

At Limehouse Police Station, the Station officer was not provided with a jailer and was therefore responsible for all the routine welfare matters relating to prisoners such as checking the cell for safety issues, providing meals and tea for them and dealing with any reasonable request, including medical attention. Not only was it a very busy role but you could be dealing with desperate people at the lowest time of their lives.

I had several close calls where prisoners attempted suicide in their cells or became ill very quickly. It was routine practice to check them in their cell at least once an hour or if they were drunk at least every 30 minutes. I had to develop a sixth sense to ensure that they were kept safe as well using all available information including taking particular notice of any warning markers on the Police National Computer (PNC) against their name. (Such as

'Violent' or 'Suicidal'). Maybe, because of good fortune I didn't have a fatal incident with a prisoner in a cell, but over the years I had some scary experiences with determined people who tried to take their own lives.

On one occasion, a young man who had been charged with a number of residential burglaries requested a phone call to his girlfriend as he was to be held in custody to go to court. I had just come on duty and I had not been informed of any potential risks. After he completed the call, I was unaware that his girlfriend had dumped him over the phone. He showed no emotion and went back to his cell quietly. It was a busy night with various comings and goings in the charge room but I had a strange feeling about the young detainee, so I decided to go and check on him in the cell. As I approached, I saw that the cell 'wicket' was open and I knew it had been closed when I left him there. The 'wicket' in this sense is a small opening on the cell door where an officer can inspect the prisoner for safety reasons before opening the door. Detained persons would often request that the 'wicket' is left open but this request is always refused by the Sergeant due to health and safety reasons. However, on occasions a constable may leave it open without permission from the sergeant, to pacify a prisoner when placing a person in a cell.

The decision to check him proved to be very important, as when I looked through the wicket I could not see him in the cell. I tried to open the door and it was unusually heavy. I suddenly realised that the man was behind the door and he was trying to take his own life by hanging himself by using the cord out of his track suit bottoms.

Luckily, I was able to open the door, call for the assistance of other officers and prevent a fatality.

Making well-reasoned decisions and being able to think on your feet are essential skills in Police work and I found that by building a rapport with offenders helped me to connect with them to understand their needs and motivation for crime. I found that too much emotion can also cloud your judgement and not to make rash decisions based on excitement. My time and experience in this role provided me with the skills that were necessary to develop informants and investigate crime more effectively later in my service.

Chapter eight

Curiosity

"The important thing is not to stop questioning. Curiosity has its own reason for existing." - Albert Einstein.

Curiosity can be defined as inquisitiveness, the tendency to ask and learn about things by asking questions, investigating or exploring.

Most people would assume that curiosity would be a natural trait of a Police officer. However, in my experience there are officers who are content to do the minimum within their role and there are others who go the extra mile because of their enthusiasm and curiosity.

Following my initiation as a Sergeant at Limehouse and Bow Police Stations I eventually 'escaped' from the duties in the charge room and I was able to patrol the streets with my colleagues on a more regularly basis. Because the Tower Hamlets area was a deprived, mainly working-class area, petty crime was rife with stolen goods being plied in public houses. Opportunist burglaries and car thefts were prevalent.

I caught the attention of senior officers because I made several arrests and encouraged junior officers to work and achieve good results. In early 1985, there was a big surge of car crime and this had an impact on the motor vehicle crime statistics in the Division. The senior managers met to discuss what action to take to combat this trend and they decided to form a small team of officers dedicated to deal with the problem.

To my surprise, I was chosen to run the plain clothes team and three constables were assigned to me. They were a varied group, with an experienced officer of 20 years' service, a 'cop' just out of his probationary period who had a big interest in cars and a 'steady' lad who had a bit of physical presence. I didn't have much of a depth of knowledge about specific cars or their performance, but I did enjoy being curious about offenders and their motivation behind the crimes.

In reality, the intention of the senior officers was for us to keep observation on areas of high crime in the hope that we would catch car thieves 'red handed'. The most prevalent crime was the theft of car radios by young people who would quickly break a car window with a hammer or even with a broken spark plug and swiftly remove the radio. Of course, in the real world, these offences happened quickly by people who were reasonably surveillance aware and therefore difficult to catch in the act. We did make a few arrests on surveillance by hiding in buildings and being fortunate to apprehend a thief who had been unaware of our presence but it was few and far between.

We apprehended suspects in the street who we found in possession of dubious car radios and articles used for 'going equipped' to steal, however, it was not always possible to trace the owner of the suspected stolen property and more often the case would not result in a charge.

I had to make the officers understand that we were in the results business and we needed to change our tactics in order to better target offenders. We had few resources and only occasional access to a Police vehicle so there was little opportunity to pursue or stop stolen vehicles and detain the car thief and therefore we tried another approach.

The area had three large car fragmentation yards (scrap yards) that accepted scrap cars for cash and I used these locations to target offenders. The principle of this approach was instead of having to rely on luck by randomly looking for suspects we would wait near the entrance to scrap yards for the car thieves to turn up with cars that they had towed from the street without permission. Sure enough, on the first day of this new approach we were waiting at a scrap yard in Tredegar Road, Bow, when a truck turned up towing an old red car that had clearly just been towed from the street. We confronted the driver of the truck and he admitted taking it from the street without making any meaningful enquiries with the owner. We arrested the driver and a passenger in the truck and took them to Limehouse Police station. I built up a rapport with them and established that they had stolen many cars by this method and scrapped them for cash at various scrap yards. My curiosity took over and we started to further investigate by visiting local yards and checking the scrap records that the owners were obliged to keep by law. We found numerous vehicles that the pair had taken off the street and scrapped. By checking the registration numbers on the records on the Police National Computer we found that many of them were reported as being stolen by their owners.

It was a goldmine of information and enquiries led to many arrests of suspects who had used similar methods to steal cars for cash by using the same 'modus operandi.' The scrap yard owners usually assisted us with our enquiries and we were never obstructed as it was in their interest to be helpful.

There were a few dead ends but we were so pro-active that the suspects started to talk openly to us and we developed several useful contacts and informants.

'Running' or handling an informant was a complex and sensitive occupation because many of them were close to people who they were informing on and they usually had more involvement in the crimes than they would admit to. For that reason, the informant had to be regularly reminded by us not to act as an 'agent provocateur'. In other words, if they set up a crime or had involvement in the commission of an offence, they would also be culpable and liable to prosecution. Informants were traditionally handled by detectives and when I was 'running' them there was always some friction and suspicion from C.I.D. even though I worked to the procedures and covered my back.

At this time, fast communication was problematic. The use of mobile phones was in its infancy and the only ones available on the market were as large as 'house bricks'. Therefore, meetings to speak with informants had to be arranged in local pubs and other public places. Any informant who provided useful information on several different occasions were officially registered and provided with pseudonyms in order to disguise their true identities from criminals and inquisitive police officers. On some occasions, if a valuable car was recovered as a direct result of their information or a serious crime was prevented, the informant received a 'pay day' from an insurance company, which was overseen officially at a Police station by a senior officer.

I did understand the sensitivity of running and protecting these informants and I always had to be curious and on my guard about their reasons for providing information to Police.

Saying this, the information that they often provided saved valuable Police time and had a substantial impact in reducing crime and detecting offenders.

Chapter nine

Tenacity

"If you fell down yesterday, stand up today." - H.G. Wells

Tenacity is the quality or fact of being very determined and therefore a tenacious person will achieve a goal or objective despite and difficulties that they encounter. It's considered a good trait to have and an essential soft skill in Police work as it can be useful when detecting and hunting down offenders.

After a couple of months with me running the motor vehicle crime squad it was time for a change or 'freshen up' of personnel. We had been quite successful as we had made many arrests for theft of motor cars by adopting the strategy of targeting fragmentation yards. Word had got round that we were being pro-active and the number of cars being taken from the street and scrapped had reduced.

Suspects who were 'on our radar' were talking to us about all sorts of criminal activity on the Borough, some were doing this to divert attention from themselves while others were doing it for reasons of revenge or even financial gain. The posting on the team was initially only for 6 weeks but because of our encouraging results I had my attachment extended. In fact, I ended up leading the team for nine months. A couple of the officers were changed and replaced by similar, enthusiastic officers who expressed an interest in working with me. I believe that I remained with the team as I provided the continuity with informants or

(CHIS – covert human intelligence source) as they later became known.

One of our long running cases came about as a result of a 'whisper' from the criminal world. We came across a high value Rolls-Royce car parked up in a small, lock up garage in Upper Clapton in north east London. Not only was it unusual to find a high value vehicle in such a location, but it was a surprise to discover that it had been reported stolen about a month or so earlier. There were no obvious signs that the car had been forcibly broken into. Our enquiries failed to give us a lead because the lock up garage had been abandoned and unlawfully used for storage. However, we were in possession of specific information that led us to believe that the 'stolen' vehicle was subject of an insurance fraud involving some local car thieves acting together with the registered owner. We urgently spoke to the insurance company and found that they were intending to pay the owner out for the loss of the vehicle but I advised them to delay payment pending our further enquiries.

We initially spoke with the registered owner of the vehicle but our suspicions regarding the removal, storage and potential disposal of the car were on a young Liverpudlian man called Theo. He lived in London and had been on the wrong side of the law for most of his life. He had an older brother called Owen, who was also suspected to have played a part in the conspiracy and had a similar antecedent's history to Theo. Owen came to prominence when he burgled an office of a politically sensitive organisation a few years before, in an attempt to steal incriminating documents. Unfortunately for Owen, he was disturbed by security officers and in an attempt to escape he fell from an upstairs window breaking his leg. He received a custodial sentence for his efforts.

Theo appeared to be the more intelligent of the two brothers and he was a much more 'slippery' character. Owen was happy to talk to us and boasted about his exploits and involvement in his part of the fraud. Theo was more difficult to trace than Owen and we discovered that he may be living with his girlfriend in a tenement block of flats in Stoke Newington, North London.

I obtained a search warrant for the flat to look for stolen goods and vehicle documents but we were unable to commit much time to surveillance prior to the search because the flat was on another Borough area.

On the morning of the 'raid' we went to the suspect address and the door was opened by a young, attractive woman whose name was Bianca. She was very nervous, defensive and denied that Theo lived with her. We made a thorough search of the flat and although Theo wasn't at home, we found numerous car log books, driving licences in different names, car keys, handwritten bills of sale and cheque books in different names in the bedroom. It was evident that some of the items were either stolen or evidence of criminal activity. We also found some men's' clothing in the wardrobe, together with documentation in Theo's name.

Bianca was taken to the Police Station and under interrogation she denied having any connection with the evidence that we found in her flat and although she told us that Theo sometimes stayed with her, she was unaware of his current whereabouts. We had to release her without charge and despite making in-depth enquiries, we were unable to trace Theo through the use of informants or official sources. Over the next couple of weeks we made several random visits to the flat, but each time we visited Theo was not there. It appeared that Theo had 'done a runner'.

In the absence of having Theo in custody, we conducted a thorough investigation into the evidence that we had recovered. It became apparent that Theo had been involved in the theft and disposal of stolen cars throughout the home counties. He was skilled in changing the identity of the cars by removing the stolen vehicles identifying features and selling them on as legitimate cars to unsuspecting buyers who paid money into his fraudulent bank accounts. In one of these fraudulent accounts, he had used Bianca's workplace address after he had found a driving licence mistakenly delivered there in the post and used it to open a bank account. We built a strong case against Theo by recovering the cars from the innocent purchasers and taking full witness statements from the victims and witnesses.

A few months went by and despite Theo's details being circulated as a wanted person on the PNC, he had not come to the attention of Police.

One afternoon, I decided to go and look for Theo again, I paired up with a woman constable who had joined the squad at the start of this particular investigation. She was tenacious like me, she had enthusiasm and a positive outlook for the job. We had some recent information that Theo was visiting Bianca again and was using a specific make of car. We had his photograph with us and although we had failed to detain him on previous attempts, we were hopeful that if we tried another method we may be successful. Our goal was to find Theo and arrest him, however unlikely that seemed after all our previous efforts. However, logically, it was probable that Theo would return to Bianca's flat at some time and we just had to be lucky to be there at the right time.

We had a small, unmarked van that we had acquired through a useful contact at the Police traffic garage. It was ideal for plain clothes duties because even the criminals didn't suspect that it was being used for Police purposes.

Instead of visiting the flat and risk missing him we waited up in the van nearby but out of view. After only a few minutes, to our surprise, we saw Theo drive out of the estate in a car and head off through the streets of Stoke Newington. He was driving at a steady speed and he had no idea that we were following him at a close distance. My colleague attempted to contact control to try and get some uniformed assistance to stop the car, but as was quite usual in those days there was radio interference and we could not get through. We followed the car for a mile or so and it became apparent that no one was going to be around to help us.

We knew that Theo was not the sort of person to give up easily as he had escaped from Police on several occasions when he had been apparently cornered. However, we realised that this was our opportunity to arrest him and our emotions were heightened as we were aware that any attempt to detain him was going to be challenging and potentially dangerous.

At this time, Stoke Newington was known to be a violent area and any arrests were often opposed by onlookers who were anti-police. Suddenly, Theo's progress was halted by a red traffic light and he found himself in a queue of traffic in Rectory Road. I knew that this was our chance to 'nab' him and I jumped out of the van and headed towards Theo who was sitting in his car on his own. Before Theo had a chance to react, I opened his car door, I shouted, "Police" and took hold of him.

Theo did his best to jump up to try and squeeze past me and run but he lost his balance and I fell on top of him in the middle of the carriageway. Theo was struggling and trying to escape but he was lighter than me and I was determined to hold onto him. My colleague joined me and assisted me to restrain Theo. Handcuffs were not general issue in these days and therefore we had to rely on our grappling and restraining techniques to hold him down. I was praying that onlookers would not get involved as we were in plain clothes and it may have appeared that we were just angry motorists, fighting in the street with an innocent man.

I had visions of him slipping through my grasp and having to pursue him on foot. My heart was racing and I was sweating due to my exertions and excitement. I refused to give up and I suppose it took me back to my days in Liverpool on foot patrol where it was just not acceptable to 'lose' a prisoner by letting him get away after detaining him. Just as I thought that things were getting too much, I saw the figure of a tall, well-built man, looming over us. I looked up at him and politely asked if he could call the Police for us. To my amazement and relief, he replied, "It's okay, I am the Police." He produced a set of gleaming handcuffs and snapped them on Theo's wrists. The man was a Detective Superintendent, who by chance had also been in the traffic queue, saw the struggle and came to our assistance. I told Theo he was under arrest for conspiracy and theft and took him to the Police Station.

Some months later, Theo appeared at Crown Court where he pleaded guilty to the charges. I noticed that his girlfriend, Bianca, was sitting in the public gallery. It transpired that Theo and Bianca were a true love story and I sometimes wonder if the couple did stay together and have a more productive and honest existence after his release from prison.

Chapter 10

Adaptability

"You cannot grow unless you are willing to change. You will never improve yourself if you cling to what used to be."-
Leon Brown

Adaptability is the quality of being able to adjust to new conditions. We all like to think of ourselves as adaptable and that we are open to change. In reality, we are more resistant to change and it is often difficult to handle. The main reason for disliking change is that most of us like routine and therefore anything that takes us out of our comfort zone presents us with a challenge.

Police officers are no different from other people when it comes to resisting change. When I was young in-service procedures and policies had remained unchanged for years and there was a continuity to the work environment. An officer's seniority, in years of service, truly meant something and usually commanded respect. Officers were also working to procedures that could be interpreted in different ways under Judges rules and there was an attitude amongst older officers that because things had been done in a certain way for many years nothing should change.

Probably the biggest change in modern Policing was the introduction of the Police and Criminal Evidence Act 1984. The legislation was brought in following the 1981 Brixton riots and the subsequent report on them by Lord Scarman. Its intention was to unify Police powers under one code of practice and to carefully balance the rights of the individual against the powers for the Police.

Prior to this legislation coming into force, solicitors and legal representatives were hardly ever seen inside a Police station and it was before the introduction of taped recorded interviews on suspects in custody. Interviews were recorded on paper by the officer without a solicitor being present and the accuracy or validity of any admissions were often called into question at court.

Investigating officers in conjunction with the Station officer Sergeant also decided on the charging decision and on some occasions, the incorrect charge was preferred. Officers were required at court much more than nowadays and they had much more say with objections to bail and other matters. When the Act came into force in 1986 the Crown Prosecution Service was formed and over the next few years they gradually took over the responsibility of deciding charging decisions and which cases should be prosecuted.

It was a huge change to Policing and many older, experienced officers found it difficult to adapt to the changing balance of power and what they perceived as the interference of the legal profession in their work.

The training that officers received initially on the new legislation was laughable. I remember being instructed to attend a training session at Arbour Square Police Station in Stepney with officers who had a variety of Police service. The training Sergeant who conducted the training looked confused and embarrassed as he tried to explain some of the more complicated new jargon. In fact, he was at a loss to communicate even the most basic parts of the act as it was all new to everyone.

Some of the more experienced detectives became frustrated and started arguing with the unfortunate Sergeant who was clearly struggling to get his point across to them. From how the older officers were talking, they believed that they could undermine the legislation because of their position and experience. I remained quiet, as I understood that this change was here to stay and as a young Sergeant I realised that we all had to adapt and move with the times.

The training Sergeant brought the session to an abrupt end, slammed the binder that contained the legislation on the table and advised us all to adjourn to the Pub. The session only lasted about 45 minutes when it had been scheduled to last for a whole day.

My knowledge of the 'workings' of the act came as a result of numerous court cases where legal brains dissected my evidence by trawling through legal books. Sometimes, my evidence was pulled apart and not accepted but in every case where I made a 'mistake' in interpreting the law I learnt something new.

When the act was officially introduced in 1986, I remember stopping a car in the street in the Limehouse area. I conducted initial checks and I became suspicious about the legality of the road fund licence. The driver of the vehicle became agitated and evasive and I decided to undertake further enquiries at the Police Station. I arrested the driver on suspicion of theft of the road fund licence and discovered from my enquiries that it had been stolen as part of a batch from a nearby Post office during a burglary.

I made a case to the duty Inspector that we should search for further stolen licences at the suspects home address and the Inspector duly authorised a search without warrant under Section 18(1) of PACE.

I went with the suspect and another officer to his home address which was similar to a lock up shop with accommodation above it. Once inside, although we didn't find any stolen road fund licences, we discovered a large quantity of power tools hidden in a cupboard. I questioned the suspect about his possession of them and he made some admissions that they were stolen property. I seized the items and returned to the Police Station. Due to practical reasons, I did not make a note of his admissions at the scene but when I returned to the Station I recorded them in my notebook and asked the suspect to sign them as being correct. The suspect had time to think about the consequences of his words and he retracted the admissions and refused to sign or accept them.

When I formally interviewed him, he made no admissions to theft and told me that he had no idea that the property was stolen and had no guilty knowledge. I conducted property checks on the power tools and somewhat surprisingly, the majority had been reported stolen and were identifiable from their serial numbers. Because of this and taking into account that I had a verbal admission and that the property was found at the suspects home address, charges of theft with an alternative of dishonestly handling stolen goods were preferred against him.

The case was heard at Southwark Crown Court and midway through my evidence there was a strong legal challenge from the defence that the admissions from the suspect that he made at the scene were inadmissible and should not be considered as evidence for the jury. Previous to the introduction of PACE the comments would have undoubtedly been accepted as part of the evidence but in this case the Judge ruled against me.

This left the jury to decide if the defendant was guilty of the crime in the absence of 'guilty knowledge' in the evidence. Remarkably the jury only took 20 minutes to decide that the defendant was guilty of receiving stolen goods and he was sentenced.

I learnt something new from my experience and rather than being resentful, I tried to look for positives in changes to the law so that I could adapt to them. I also found that it was important to look and listen to the experiences of other officers and try and learn from them so that I could be more effective and a better role model for younger constables.

Chapter eleven

Emotional intelligence

"When awareness is brought to an emotion, power is brought to your life." - Tara Meyer Robson

Emotional intelligence is as important as intellectual intelligence. It can help you manage your emotions in a positive way. It also helps you recognise your own emotional state and the emotional state of others. Emotional intelligence can enable you to develop good relationships with others, be successful at work and achieve your goals. There are four key abilities in the soft skill.

1. Self-awareness - this is the ability to understand your own emotions and how they can affect your thoughts and emotions.

2. Self-management - this is the ability to control feelings and behaviour and adapt to changes.

3. Social -awareness - the ability to understand the emotions and concerns of other people and recognise the power dynamics in a group organisation.

4. Relationship management - This is the ability to build and maintain good relations, communicate clearly, inspire and influence others, work well in a team and manage conflict.

As you can see from the above, emotional intelligence is a key soft skill for a police officer to possess and develop in order to interact with colleagues and the general public effectively.

Back in 1986, I had been a Police Sergeant for four years and I felt that I was gaining respect from my colleagues, by leading from the front and being prepared to guide and encourage others to work in a similar manner. I had recently returned to response duties after running a successful crime squad and I had impressed senior officers by the way I had cultivated informants and managed my team.

I was approached one day by an Inspector who told me that the Superintendent wanted me to become the supervisor for the Home Beat officers. I was somewhat surprised at this request, because I was developing a reputation as a pro-active leader whilst the Home Beats officers were generally viewed as work-shy older constables who had been 'put out to grass' and who had other outside interests that took 'precedence' over their Police duties.

However, the request from above was non-negotiable as many other that came from senior officers to subordinates back in the day.

I was allowed a couple of weeks grace before having to take over the responsibilities from the outgoing sergeant. I took the opportunity to meet up with him and have a coffee and a chat. I had been stationed at Bow Police station for some time on the response team and therefore I had witnessed some of the home beat officers 'drifting' in and out of the station office and apparently failing to produce any tangible results. The sergeant was rarely on duty because he had a particular job specialism that meant he was often working from other Police stations, leaving his officers unsupervised. Consequently, several of the constables became demotivated and there were strong rumours amongst response officers that some home beat officers were not even reporting for work or going missing on duty.

After the meeting with the sergeant, I was aware that there was tension developing within the home beat team because the outgoing sergeant was well liked and there was a feeling amongst them that I was coming in to sort them out. This rumour had been created by some response team officers who had been talking to the home beat officers intimating that I had an agenda to get some of them moved off the team. The truth was that I was going in with an open mind and did not want to rush to judgements, as I was willing to give everyone a chance rather than making assumptions on what I had heard from others.

On my first day in charge, I decided to hold a brief meeting with all the officers together. I was feeling slightly apprehensive but I was determined to hide my emotions and stay calm, so I went there with the intention of having a fairly low-key introductory chat.

The home beat 'team' gathered in an office for the meeting and I immediately became aware that there were two separates 'cliques' in the group. Maybe it would be more accurate to call it one clique in fact. When I used the term 'team' nothing could be further from the truth. Officers were assigned to a beat on a permanent basis and from what I could see there was little or no teamwork.

The clique comprised of five male officers who were in mid service and appeared to intimidate the other officers, who were mostly younger and less experienced. I could feel the resentment towards me from the clique of older officers and a feeling of expectation from the others.

Following personal introductions from everyone, I gave a brief outline for my plans going forward, choosing my words carefully and hopefully wisely. Nothing in my address was particularly controversial, but I could feel the apparent resistance from the clique, that gradually turned to frustration and exasperation. I let the officers have their say and it became obvious that the clique of older officers were 'not on board' with my proposals whilst the younger officers became more confident and vocal. I ended the meeting with half of the group being disgruntled and distant and the others feeling hopeful and inspired.

The first couple of months were a challenge but not without success as I gave everyone the opportunity to achieve success whilst I observed their strengths and weaknesses. However, the older clique of officers continued to be resentful towards my position on the team. Although they were turning up for duty and patrolling the streets, the atmosphere with them in the office was 'frosty' and uncomfortable.

I knew that something was going to give and I was determined it was not going to be me on the receiving end. I looked at myself honestly to ensure that I was giving everyone the same opportunities and challenges.

It's always difficult to motivate people who are unwilling to change and it became a battle of wits and emotions. I was appreciated by the younger group of officers because I remained professional and pro-active. I should say that I don't believe that the older officers were bad and I am sure that most of them had done some good work during their careers but they were being unwilling to move forward. Their lack of flexibility and emotional intelligence put them in a position that was difficult for them to get out of. But the situation suddenly changed due to an unforeseen incident.

I came into work one morning and was informed by a senior officer that two of my constables had been involved in an off-duty incident with a member of the public and had been suspended from work. It never good to hear something of this nature but in a strange way it turned out to be a positive. The two officers involved in the incident were probably the most disruptive members of the clique and ended up being off work for some time, before being moved off the team completely. Of the other three officers, one of them decided to resign from the MPS and seek other employment and the remaining two were successful in transferring to other roles within the Police away from the team.

I was then in a position to encourage more pro-active officers on to the team to join me. They had the opportunity to be flexible with their duties and work on their own initiative as long as they were professional and demonstrated a good work ethic.

Gradually, I was able to change the perception of the role and I started to mould the individuals into a team and achieve some excellent outcomes.

Chapter twelve

Teamwork

"Alone we can do so little; together we can do so much." - Helen Keller

There is a lot written about the mechanics of teamwork and people with business acumen have developed companies that are intended to train corporate managers and employees with the techniques of building a team.

There is a good reason for this because an effective team of people working together to achieve a common goal can be far more productive than individuals working to their own plan. It stands to reason, in the modern working environment following the covid 19 pandemic with more people working from home, it can be challenging for managers to supervise and for employees to maintain focus.

The definition of teamwork is 'The combined action of a group, especially when effective and efficient.' There are many inspirational quotes bandied about on the subject, such as 'T.E.A.M. - together everyone achieves more', 'teamwork makes the dream work' and 'the nicest thing about teamwork is that you always have others on your side'.

Whilst these quotes are nice to have framed and hung on the office wall, building a team and promoting teamwork is a lot more complicated. I believe that managers would do better to remember adopting John Adair's, 'Action centred approach' in order to maintain balance in a group. 'Team – task- Individual'. Adair was a Scots Guard who became a senior lecturer at Sandhurst, and he developed this model. The reason to remember this mantra is that sometimes managers can get fixated on the task in hand and neglect the importance of the individual and his/her contribution to the team.

A few months after the departure of the disgruntled older officers on the home beat team, the newly recruited constables were settling in and were working in harmony with the other officers who remained from the original personnel. I had achieved a good balance of experience and energetic young officers who had innovative ideas. The common thread was they all had enthusiasm and were working and helping each other with a positive attitude. I was pleased to have them because the hardest thing about being a leader is when you have individuals who have poor attitudes and are cynical about their role.

I constantly reminded my team that our purpose was to provide high visibility patrolling to reassure the public, engage with the community to understand their concerns, develop trust and take effective enforcement action against offenders. To do this meant that they had responsibility for their own beats and develop a network of contacts in partnership with agencies such as schools, the local authority and community groups.

I held regular team meetings to agree and define clear goals and to review our progress with ongoing community issues. I found that when I briefed the team I would try and keep instructions straight-forward with simplicity being the key to success so that everyone, irrespective of length of service or experience could understand the objective. By doing this I would concentrate their minds on one task. Whether it was to look for a stolen car or a missing person or to take part in a particular community initiative. I realised that by doing this the goal was usually achieved rather than giving an individual several random tasks and ending up with achieving nothing. I used to emphasise that if each of us achieve one success, however small, each week, the cumulative result over the course of a year would be substantial.

At one of these meetings, the officer who patrolled the Bromley-by-Bow area mentioned that he had become aware that there had been a spate of residential burglaries in three high-rise blocks in Rainhill Way. It was quite concerning as many of the flats were occupied by female nurses who worked shifts at the nearby St Andrews Hospital. He told us that the burglaries were taking place in the daytime and on one occasion a flat was forcibly entered where an off-duty nurse was asleep in bed. The C.I.D. had not identified this pattern of crime as they were apparently dealing with more serious issues and they asked us to look into the matter. At this time, the C.I.D. appeared to underestimate us as a crime fighting unit and still referred to us a 'wooden-tops'. This was a derogatory term used by the C.I.D. to describe beat officers.

I put the officer who had identified the problem in charge of the operation and delegated others to take witness statements and make house to house enquiries. I also directed officers to patrol as a team in the vicinity of the crimes with an evidenced based approach, keep an open mind and use their powers where necessary. From my experience with a spate of burglaries such as this one, it was likely that the offender or offenders lived nearby as there was no information about a vehicle being used and some of the stolen property was bulky.

Officers soon came back with useful information about the descriptions of the offenders that they had obtained from witnesses. This information was corroborated thanks to a stop and search on a tall, athletic, young man, a day or so earlier, who I had found in possession of a black bin sack in his pocket. Although it was an innocent article on its own, taking into account the information that we had obtained vital information from our enquiries, it became apparent that the bag was probably to be used for conveying stolen property through the streets following a break in.

We applied to Thames Magistrates Court for a search warrant at the home address of the main suspect with the intention of executing it as soon as possible. I made preparations to assemble a search team and my officers were willing to change their duty times to achieve a good result for an interesting job.

The next morning, we met in the office and the officer in charge of the operation briefed everyone about the purpose and objective of the raid. I delegated specific roles to everyone present and we made our way to the suspect's home.

On our arrival the front door, it was opened by a middle-aged black woman who turned out to be the suspect's mother. She was understandably surprised with our early morning call but after she was presented with a copy of the search warrant, she was very compliant. Unfortunately, her son was not at home and the woman showed us to her son's bedroom. He had a single room but on entering it was obvious that it was packed full of stolen property. We had a list of items that had been stolen from the burglaries, complete with serial numbers and we set about identifying a stolen television, a video recorder, expensive cameras, jewellery and other readily identifiable property such as cheque books and driving licences.

The woman was visibly shocked with the discovery of the property and provided us with information about her son's friends who we also suspected of being involved in the burglaries and receiving stolen goods. We seized all the stolen property and asked the woman to speak to her son and get him to attend the Police station when he returned home. Within a few hours the suspect presented himself at the front desk of the Police station where we interviewed him under arrest.

When confronted with our evidence, he openly confessed to carrying out four residential burglaries and also implicated two other youths who had assisted him. Needless to say, our enquiries led us to the arrest of the other two youths and the recovery of more stolen property.

We returned the stolen items to their rightful owners and three suspects received two years in custody each for their crimes.

This was an excellent example of teamwork with everyone playing their part to ensure that the suspects were arrested and brought to justice.

Chapter thirteen

Cultural awareness

"The beauty of the world lies in the diversity of its people."
- unknown

Someone's cultural awareness is the understanding of the differences between themselves and people from other countries or other backgrounds, especially differences in attitudes and values.

London is one of the most diverse cities in the world with over 300 languages being spoken. This diversity has come about as a result of industrialisation and the growing British empire. This meant that people from all over the world were trading in London by the 1800s and the population grew rapidly.

Tower Hamlets in London is the fourth linguistically diverse area in England and Wales with at least 90 different languages being spoken and where a third of all adults use a main language other than English. The borough has a rich history of immigrant communities settling there and the evidence of this is reflected by the buildings and the street names. In the 1680s the Huguenots from France settled in the Brick Lane area and worked in the silk weaving industry. Soon after, the Jewish community came to the Borough from Russia and stayed well into the 1930s before dispersing to other areas of London.

After the second world war West Indians from the 'Windrush' generation came to London in search of work with many of them working on London Transport.

Further back in the 1860s the Chinese came to the area and settled around Limehouse causeway and the first 'Chinatown' was developed there. They originally came here as sailors who docked at West India Docks and stayed with their families and started businesses. The traditional Chinese food and the restaurants became very popular although there was a more sinister aspect to their community with the open use of hard drugs in 'Opium dens'. The Chinese mostly relocated to the Soho area of London and the void was filled by the Bangladeshi community from Sylhet. The Bengali's became the biggest immigrant community and now make up 30% of the population in Tower Hamlets.

Respecting diversity and having cultural awareness are now essential qualities or skills for modern day Police officers and considerable training is provided to them. In addition, great efforts have been made to recruit people from ethnic minorities to become Police officers, although they continue to be under-represented.

Of course, having such a diverse population can result in tensions between communities especially in times of economic depression when immigrants can be seen as scapegoats and the reason for the bad state of the country. In 1936, the Jewish community were targeted by the fascist 'Blackshirt' movement and the battle of Cable Street took place in the Shadwell area of Tower Hamlets. There have also been street riots such as the Brixton riots in 1981 where the predominant West Indian community fought back at what they perceived to be unfair and insensitive policing. Subsequently, the Scarman report was produced which led to major changes in law and Police procedures.

The McPherson report was published following the murder of Stephen Lawrence in 1993 and defined that the MPS was 'institutionally racist' following the bungled investigation into his death. More recently the Black Lives Matter (BLM) movement have shone a light on equality issues and social justice for people of colour.

It's important to learn from others and read about history in order to discover about different customs, culture and diversity.

Despite these high-profile cases being reported by the media, it is important to remember that there are many instances of excellent Police work bringing racially motivated criminals to book across the MPS and county Police forces.

During my first attachment to the Bow Home beat team in 1988 we set up one of the first racial incident panels in the MPS. We worked closely with Housing officers from the local authority and periodically reviewed cases where allegations had been made of racial harassment and crime by residents. This was before the time of specific legislation relating to racially motivated offences. The Bangladeshi community had settled mostly in the E1 postcode area around Whitechapel and Shadwell. Bow in East London was an area that was mainly occupied by the white majority but there was a small number of the Bangladesh community being moved into Council property by the Local Authority. They were isolated in their Council accommodation and sometimes they were targeted by criminal members of the white majority who were resentful about their culture and religious differences.

One day, the officer on my team, who was responsible for Policing the Roman Road area mentioned that a crime had been committed and it had not received the attention that it warranted. He was an officer who had an eye for details and a sense of fair play. A Bangladeshi family, who had been harassed by residents in a large council owned estate called, Lefevre Walk, had suffered a burglary where the offenders had violently assaulted the elder male resident inside the property in front of his family. The suspects, who were white, had used weapons and the victim was quite badly injured. I instructed the officer to obtain full written statements from the victim and witnesses through an official interpreter because English was not their first language. Then we did a series of house-to-house enquiries. Unfortunately, we were met with a wall of silence even though the crime must have been witnessed by local people because it was committed in broad daylight and the front door of the flat had been kicked in. CCTV was not a crime prevention tool that was often available in the late 1980s and without conclusive forensic evidence, identification of the suspects was unlikely.

It felt as though there were no more avenues to explore but then we had an unexpected breakthrough. A concerned resident contacted us and gave the names of two young men who he told us had been involved in the crime. The resident refused to provide a written statement as he feared repercussions but gave information that only a witness to the incident would have known. We

70

conducted checks on the names provided to us and found that they were both 'known to Police'. They were both white 'skinheads' and both of them had previously been involved in violent unprovoked encounters with Asian people.

We believed that we had sufficient grounds to arrest and question them on suspicion, so we conducted an early morning raid on their addresses. Fortunately, they were both at home and we made a search of their rooms. We found clothing inside that the victim had described in their statements together with an array of weapons. As a result of careful questioning together with the evidence that we found at the addresses, both of them admitted that they had taken part in the crime, had forced entry and assaulted the tenant. They showed no remorse and there did not appear to be any other motive other than that the victims were Asian people.

Both of them were arrested and charged with committing aggravated burglary and a few months later the two suspects appeared at the Central Criminal Court (The Old Bailey) where they were found guilty to the offences charged.

The presiding Judge was unimpressed with their behaviour and sentenced them both to two years in prison. Senior officers recognised the investigation as being exceptional work and we were presented with framed commendations. This was quite unusual for this type of case as commendations were often given to detectives for investigative work but not to uniform officers. However, we were happy to accept them of course.

Nowadays, modern society is more inclusive and we can all celebrate religious festivals such as Eid and Diwali in addition to our more traditional holidays. Cultural foods and recipes also bring tend to people together and provide a focal point. This can help with community cohesion and reduce tensions at times of stress.

Chapter fourteen

Social intelligence

"Your work is the single greatest means at your disposal for expressing your social intelligence." - Robert Greene

Social intelligence develops from experience with people and learning from success and failures in social settings. It is more commonly referred to as common sense. The key difference between social and emotional intelligence is the ability to recognise one's own and others' feelings of emotional intelligence, whereas social intelligence is the ability to understand and interact with other people.

I have always been fascinated with people's lives and careers and despite being quite shy in my youth, I developed into quite a social animal. Increasing my interactions improved my verbal fluency and conversational skills. I believe I was fortunate to have worked in a variety of job settings that gave me a good grounding to deal with a variety of people from all backgrounds.

Before I joined the Police, I was employed on the M.C.C. staff as a young cricketer at Lords Cricket Ground in North West London. As an employee, I was expected to be a team player and deliver excellent customer service to club members and the general public. I met a wide range of people from different back grounds. One minute you may be talking to a group of young men on a day out from the east end of London and the next you could be conversing with a celebrity or member of parliament in the Long Room of the Pavilion.

I taught myself to be a good listener in order to prevent any misunderstandings and to protect the reputation of the iconic institution. Consequently, I became comfortable in most social environments and developed a skill of being capable of 'summing up' the behaviour and character of individuals quickly. These skills were helpful when I joined the Police as I was able to read a person's character and when I was part of a team I could work out what 'makes people tick.'

To me, social intelligence is being able to converse with all types of people using empathy, listening skills and always having an open mind to others point of view. I used social intelligence when cultivating informants, dealing with people at public meetings, speaking with victims of crime and generally conversing with the general public in non-confrontational situations.

Our networking skills as the Home Beat Team at Bow was building trust between the Police and the public. In addition to our daily duties, we also organised several charity events to raise money for local and National causes. One of the events that we organised was a charity team run from Liverpool Docklands and the London Docklands that we called the 'Heart to Heart run'. Both of these areas were emerging as new and vibrant places for living and working and we were keen to showcase them by visiting Police forces throughout the country on route. We were fortunate enough to obtain backing from several local businesses who donated the use of a vehicle together with drinks and some cash towards the cause. We raised a considerable amount of money for the British Heart Foundation charity and raised the profile of our team. This demonstrated to local people that we were committed to improving the welfare of the community and our pro-active policing style encouraged local residents to become involved in helping us. Even the local criminals noticed the change to the area that we were making and we were gaining respect from all sorts of people inside and outside of the job.

There was an interesting case at about this time involving two youths who I will refer to as Simon and Ryan. They were brothers who lived in a council house off Devons Road in Bow and both were prolific car thieves. We regularly came into contact with them and we often arrested them for driving offences and car theft. They had connections to a local scrap yard where cars were repaired or broken up for parts. Simon was about 18 years old and the younger of the two. Although he was a recidivist, he rarely became involved in physical violence whereas Ryan, was older and was of large build. He had a reputation of fighting and had been arrested for more serious crime.

When I apprehended them, I always treated them fairly and they appeared to respect this approach. Their father was known to Police in his younger days as being involved in petty crime and he had an 'old school' attitude with his relationship with law enforcement. Me and the home beat team became quite well known as local officers and I had a connection to this particular area as both my parents had been born and bred there.

One day, I was in the office at Bow Police Station, when two detectives came in. One of them was a local officer and the other was from a specialist unit at Scotland Yard. They explained to me that there had been a serious incident in Stoke Newington where four males had paid a 'visit' to an opposing scrap yard and randomly fired shots using what they believed was a machine gun and a shotgun. It was suspected of being a revenge attack and during a barrage of gunshots, a dog was shot and killed. They feared that the dispute between the men was escalating and becoming more violent.

To my surprise two of the men involved were named as Simon and Ryan. The detectives asked me for as much information that I could give on them as they were not only looking to arrest them but they also wanted to recover the firearms.

I was of course aware that Simon and Ryan were petty criminals but I did not think that they would ever resort to using firearms. However, I provided all relevant information about them and I, along with other officers, were invited onto the investigation.

The next morning the home addresses of the suspects were raided by armed Police and detectives from Scotland yard. I went with officers to assist at Simons and Ryan's home. Three of the four suspects were arrested including Ryan. Simon lived in the same house but was not at home. The other two suspects were detained at other addresses. The detectives at the scene with Ryan, questioned their parents forcefully, almost bordering on aggression. The father was not forthcoming with any useful information, having been understandably disorientated with having their house raided by Police, armed with guns and dressed in combat wear. Suddenly, the father saw me in the crowd of cops gathered in the dimly lit hallway of the house. He pointed at me in the relief of seeing a 'friendly' face and requested to speak to me in confidence. He knew me from previous dealings with his sons and recognised that I was honest and trustworthy. He named one of the men who had been arrested as being the ringleader and he suspected that this man had obtained the guns that were used on the job. He also told me where Simon was likely to be hiding and he asked the detectives if I could go with them to the address. He realised that my presence would probably reduce any conflict at the scene.

I went with the detectives and we arrested Simon in a room in a hostel in Cadogan Terrace near Victoria Park. Although we did not recover a firearm, we found some shotgun cartridges under the mattress of the bed where he had been sleeping.

During that same day, I received information from residents who had been appalled at the shooting and wanted to help. The firearms were never recovered but Simon and Ryan were charged with conspiracy to assault and were held in custody.

Both of them pleaded guilty to the charges at the Old Bailey and were sentenced to 15 years in prison between them.

The majority of our work as home beat officers was routine and relatively minor in nature. But by developing trust and continuity with the public and by using good social intelligence skills, it demonstrates that even serious crime can be prevented and detected.

Chapter fifteen

Observation skills

"All of us are watchers – of television, of time clocks, on traffic on the freeway – but few are observers. Everyone is looking, not many are seeing." - Peter M. Leschak

Observation skills refer to the ability to use all five of your senses to recognise, analyse and recall your surroundings. Developing proper observational skills is not only necessary, but crucial for a Police officer. When I talk about this skill I'm not talking about directed or intrusive surveillance that are commonly referred to as 'Observations'. These activities are now fully covered by recent legislation under the Regulation of Investigatory Powers Act. I am concentrating on developing the basic skills of a patrolling officer to prevent crime and enforce the law.

Developing the ability to observe means learning to change specific habits. For example, it is about thinking like a criminal and looking for the unusual. This could be an understanding a suspicious person's body language or maybe recognising that an unusual item is being held or carried by an individual.

Often criminals identify their victims in poorly lit areas or side streets where there is no CCTV coverage. In order to properly observe, an officer who is patrolling in a car must not drive faster than 15mph as at a greater speed it is difficult to understand and react to what has been observed.

On occasions, when I was in the MPS, area car crews consisted of a driver, whose role was self-explanatory, and an operator, who communicated over the radio set and recorded incidents. Resources permitting, the crew could be enhanced with an observer, who was deployed in plain clothes and used to spot potential crimes or unusual behaviour. A good observer could produce excellent results by not just watching but looking and paying attention to the surroundings. Unfortunately, nowadays, from my own experience, it appears that a lot of patrolling officers are driven by response times, to the increasing number of emergency calls, resulting in Police vehicles being driven at high speeds. Drivers and operators are often engaged with in-car computers, mobile devices and phones. Although these devices may be necessary in modern policing, in order to develop your observational skills it is essential to avoid distractions.

This skill is also dependant on other attributes such as communication, emotional intelligence, critical thinking and attention to detail. The latter is very important when observing a suspect's description. I often found it difficult to recall a suspects clothing, so therefore I developed my skills by looking for details such as a person's tattoo, scar or unusual physical feature that could not be readily changed. Clothing can easily be removed and discarded but physical features can produce a positive and indisputable identification. I would also advise that you quantify things as you notice them and be specific when you make a written note of a suspects first description.

Met Police Commissioners periodically come and go and they bring with them their own new ideas and policies. Sir Peter Imbert was the boss of the Met (1987-1992) and he instigated a project called 'The Plus Programme'. The thrust behind it was to create a better organisation with improved customer service and eliminate the 'us and them' culture.

I remember attending a one-day course at Wapping Police Station on the banks of the Thames and being in a classroom with a cleaner, a garage mechanic, a canteen woman and a marine maintenance man. The course was intended to break down barriers between Police officers and Police staff. The programme did go some way to achieving the objectives, however, there were casualties along the way. One of them was that there was a shake up with community Policing at the time and I found myself back on shift work, on a response team or 'relief' performing custody office duties and responding to 999 calls when I was out on the street.

I had developed new skills whilst on the Home Beat team and I was determined to pass them on to my colleagues.

One night duty, I had finished my refreshments at 2am and I was patrolling in a 'Panda car' with a constable called Chas who was driving. I always believed that time management and punctuality were important qualities and so we were out at 2am on the dot. Chas was an 'enthusiastic' driver and I politely asked him to slow his speed down so that we could observe properly for any suspicious or criminal activity.

It was a quiet night and we weren't rushing to a call, we were both conversing with each other but we did not let this small talk distract us from looking for crime. It was a dark night as there was no moon and we patrolled the main roads and north side of Victoria Park. As we passed a side street adjacent to a large Council estate called the Ranwell Estate, I noticed some movement in the darkness and the sound of male voices close to a social club that was about 50 yards down the side street. I wasn't 100% sure of what I had seen and I told Chas to stop the car so that we could investigate. We drove into the side street, which was poorly lit and we saw two figures loitering in the shadows. Their presence was highly suspicious because the social club was closed for business and there was no reason for anyone to be hanging about there at that time of the morning.

We got out of our car and the two figures walked away from us at the side of the club. We confronted them and saw they were two white males in their 20's who both looked very nervous and furtive. We asked them what they were doing and why were they there and initially they were evasive and vague. They tried to explain that they were just going to the loo but on examination of the area there was no evidence of this. While I was talking to them, I noticed that there was a strong smell of petrol on their clothing and I made the decision to search them as they were both wearing long coats with deep pockets.

Their behaviour turned from being nervous to being visibly agitated and on searching one of them I felt a glass object and a soft cloth in his coat. I pulled the items out of his coat pocket and found a bottle together with a box of matches. On closer inspection of the bottle, I saw that there was a white cloth stuffed in the neck of the bottle and it was secured with some tape. The bottle was about a third full of petrol. The male confessed that both of them had made a petrol bomb and come there with the intention of burning down the club.

Both men were detained and arrested and taken to the Police Station for further investigation. When they were formally interviewed, they both admitted their part in a conspiracy to cause arson as their intent was to destroy the club by fire. It was only our intervention at the intended scene of the crime that prevented them to carrying out the substantive crime. They explained that their motive was revenge, as they were part of a music band who had played a gig at the club a fortnight before. There was a dispute after the gig between themselves and members of the committee, who refused to pay them. Instead of seeking compensation through a legal route, the two men made a misguided decision to return to the club and teach the committee a lesson, intending to use a petrol bomb to burn down the club by throwing it through a window.

Their plan backfired when they were observed loitering in the street and our swift action prevented the destruction of the club itself. Both men pleaded guilty at court and received custodial sentences. This incident provides an example of proactive, patrolling police using their senses and being alert to prevent a serious crime.

Chapter sixteen

Communication

"Communication is a skill that you can learn. It's like riding a bicycle or typing. If you're willing to work at it, you can rapidly improve the quality of your life." - Brian Tracy

Communication can be defined as the imparting or exchanging of information by speaking, writing or using some other medium.

The subject of communication is very complex and therefore may have too many points to cover in a small chapter. Therefore, I have summarised the skill subject by concentrating on the main pitfalls and also how to improve yourself as an effective communicator.

Communication has three parts. The sender encodes the message, the message is then transmitted, usually by speech or writing and the recipient decodes it. There are different categories of communication.

1. Spoken communication - such as face to face, telephone or by media.

2. Non-verbal- such as body language or how we dress or act.

3. Written- such as letter, reports, emails, books, internet or other media.

4. Visualisations – such as maps, logos, graphs and charts.

In policing it is important to use appropriate language when communicating and ensure that you take time before you speak. It is essential that you do not offend and always be aware of the effect your words may have on others. You should treat everyone with respect and develop the skill of being able to adapt your conversation to the audience. Remember that the use of police acronyms (e.g., IC3, RTC etc.) may not be readily understood by the general public.

Body language is usually recognised by our instinctive methods of decoding that we have subconsciously developed during our lifetime. Maybe surprising, we send off more messages with our body language than we do with the spoken word. Recognising signals and facial expressions of a potential aggressor can be useful to spot danger and the manner in which we behave can reduce conflict. It is worth investing some time to develop our knowledge of body language and always remember to actively listen.

Written communication can be a real skill in itself and is a necessity for all Police officers. All reports, letters, emails etc. must be phrased properly and concisely using good grammar and correct spelling. My advice is that before you submit any report, check it through for mistakes or language that may cause offence to avoid embarrassment. This is especially important when sending emails and messages over mobile phones, so ensure you check the message through before you hit the send button.

The desired outcome of any communication is mutual understanding and it is vital to receive feedback from the recipient that they have understood the message. This is important when transmitting a message over the personal radio. The NATO alphabet should be used when spelling out words and registration numbers of vehicles.

Now more than ever, interpreters are being employed to communicate formally with people whose first language is not English or who have speech or hearing difficulties. It's important to note that although it's sufficient to use a member of the public to translate at times of urgency, an official, registered interpreter should be used if the case is going to court.

On occasions, Police have to use innovative measures to communicate effectively with a person as I outline in the following example.

I was on patrol in a marked Police car with a fellow Sergeant. It was a weekday evening and I was back on a response team in preparation to joining the crime squad in 1989. It was quite dark and we were patrolling the side streets around Poplar High Street in Limehouse. My colleague was always a busy Police officer whose strengths were in the area of 'stop and search' and he often produced good results finding people in possession of illegal drugs and weapons. I found him to be an interesting person to work with and our individual skills complemented each other.

We were in general conversation when we saw a young woman standing on the pavement trying to get our attention. The woman was white, of slim build and in her late teens. She was an attractive woman but she had a panic-stricken expression on her face and she was waving her arms erratically. We stopped next to her to find out what, if anything, had happened to her. Before we had a chance to speak, she started to try and communicate with us by making loud, gasping noises and she was pointing in the direction of an estate in Poplar High Street. It was impossible to understand anything she was trying to tell us and we attempted to establish if she was ill or injured in any way. She was visibly upset and she was getting exasperated with us because she could not get her message across. We calmed her down by giving gentle reassurance and allowed her to sit in the Police vehicle with us for her own safety. We became aware from her actions and body language that she had severe speech and hearing difficulties. Neither me or my colleague had any useful knowledge of British sign language, so I handed her a pen and paper and asked her questions by writing them down and waiting for a reply when she had written it.

In short, she told us that she had been assaulted by four teenage boys of Bangladeshi appearance, who had physically taken hold of her and touched her intimate parts. She communicated to us that they were in a nearby estate and that she would be able to identify them. The communication process was slow and required patience but we gained her trust and confidence. In this type of case, time is of the essence and she agreed to come with us in order to point them out.

Within a minute or so we pulled into the estate and we saw four boys of a similar description standing in the doorway of a block of flats. The woman became loud and animated and pointed at the youths as if to identify them as being the suspects. Me and my colleague approached the group and our quick actions took them by surprise. They could see the woman in the Police car and heard her shouting. One of the youths immediately shouted out words to the effect that he had not been responsible for the attack and that the other three had assaulted her. We called for back-up and we managed somehow to keep them apart so that they could not speak or confer with each other. By the time that support had arrived, three of the youths had made significant statements implicating each other in what amounted to a serious sexual assault. We recorded the statements in our notebooks which the suspects agreed with and signed them as a correct record. All four of them were taken to the Police Station for further investigation.

The woman turned out to live on the estate and was later able to supply a full written statement with the help of an official interpreter. The youths were all interviewed by detectives and thanks to our innovative method of communication at the scene, they admitted their guilt in the indecent assault of a vulnerable woman.

Chapter seventeen

Leadership

"A leader is one who knows the way, goes the way and shows the way." - John Maxwell

A definition of leadership is the action of leading a group of people or organisation.

Sometimes, it easier to demonstrate this skill by talking about bad or incompetent leadership. Let's face it, anyone who has worked in a team or a workplace will complain about a manager who provides poor direction or leadership. This usually comes down to a number of factors including a lack of clear direction, a lack of honesty and inconsistency when dealing with problems.

At the extreme end of the scale, I have witnessed poor leadership during the Broadwater Farm riots in Tottenham, North London on the evening of 6th October 1985. I was on night duty at this time at Bow Police Station and the riot was taking place a few miles away. The disturbances were triggered by a combination of issues including the death of two black women in separate incidents during Police searches of their homes. Tension was running high in the Tottenham area and violence between Police and youths had escalated during the day. Police tried to clear the streets but youths responded with bricks and petrol bombs resulting in many injuries as well as extensive damage to property and vehicles. The main conflict took place in the centre of the Broadwater Farm estate and two Police officers were treated for gunshot wounds.

At about 9.30pm Police and Fire brigade responded to reports of a fire in a block called Tangmere House on the estate. The officers who were assigned to assist the Fire fighters were less well equipped and less well prepared for dealing with disorder. One of the officers was P.C. Keith Blakelock. The Police were ambushed by rioters who murdered P.C. Blakelock in a frenzied attack using knives and machetes. The chaotic incident and terror from the officers' voices on the scene was communicated over the radio system which I was listening to in the front office at Bow Police Station. I clearly remember junior officers screaming abuse over the airwaves at the senior officers who were in charge of the operation at the lack of clear leadership.

Subsequently, it was identified that there was a lack of communication through the ranks and a lack of clarity of who was in operational charge.

This is an extreme example of poor leadership in the Police but I am sure we all have our own accounts of poor decision making in our respective roles.

Leadership is a skill that can be developed. It is a journey and we must remember our previous experiences and learn from our mistakes. It's important that we review our strategies and adapt them where necessary.

At the end of the 1980s, I was posted as a Sergeant in charge of the Crime Squad at Limehouse Police Station under the direction of a new Detective Chief Inspector (D.C.I.). He was a larger-than-life character and an inspirational leader. In his younger days he had been a keen sportsman who had competed at international level. I believe that he had recognised my potential and enthusiasm for the job and he had seen me develop the home beat team into an effective crime fighting unit. During my time of being attached to the Crime squad, my officers made arrests for offences including drug dealing, serious assault and theft as a result of our pro-active approach to patrolling. We were also involved in the investigation of two separate murders where the suspects were later arrested and charged.

The D.C.I. was like a breath of fresh air in the C.I.D. and he had come from a uniformed background. He gave clear direction and was a catalyst for change in the department.

At this time in my service, Police had to deal with a new crime trend in the form of illegal warehouse parties or 'acid house'. They were usually held in large, abandoned warehouses on an impromptu basis and they attracted large numbers of people. There was usually a prevalence of illegal drug use at the events with partygoers using substances such as ecstasy. The events were advertised by word of mouth, making it difficult for Police to prepare and intervene in sufficient numbers to close them down. As time went on Police became more aware of the identity of the organisers and the possible locations where the raves were going to be held. Therefore, they became more adept at breaking them up at an early stage.

Information was received by the D.C.I. that one of these parties was to take place on a chartered boat which was due to leave from the pier at Cuba Street on the Isle of Dogs. There were obvious health and safety risks for this type of event and it would also be impossible to detect drug dealing on the boat if it set sail along the Thames.

The D.C.I. had a good understanding of the MPS and he had many useful contacts. He managed to assemble about 100 officers from various units throughout London and brought them together for an urgent briefing. He was not afraid to make brave decisions and delegate responsibility to trustworthy officers.

He took the briefing himself and he clearly set out the goals and objectives of the operation. He intended us to board the boat at Cuba Street when it was about to sail, then for us to stop the event and arrest the drug dealers on board. He had so much clarity and belief that I had no doubt that we would be successful.

However, things don't always go to plan in the real world and he received news that the venue for the start of the event had been unexpectedly changed from Cuba Street to Greenwich which was on the other side of the river Thames. The D.C.I. reassured us that he had forward-planned that there may be a change of venue and he calmly communicated this to all of us.

He instructed us to get in the Police vehicles and we made our way through the Blackwall Tunnel to Greenwich. On arrival, the D.C.I. gathered us all together in a nearby side street and gave us final verbal instructions before we boarded the boat via a gangway.

There were crowds of young people on board the boat and we all followed our individual roles. I went to the control room of the boat as requested and I searched the 'Captain' for illegal drugs. He did not have any drugs on him but I subsequently arrested him for an unrelated offence.

I became aware that various 'party-goers' had been arrested after being searched for illegal substances.

The execution of the raid had been perfect, the party was stopped and the main suspects had been arrested. The D.C.I. held a debrief for everyone back at Limehouse Police Station and congratulated us for a job well done. A suspect, who had previously been identified as the main dealer, had been arrested for possession of illegal drugs with intent to supply and he was later sentenced at court for a substantial period of imprisonment.

I learnt a lot from working with this D.C.I. and will always remember the three main roles in leadership.

1. Leaders need to give clear goals and objectives.

2. Leaders need to motivate staff and supply direction.

3. Leaders should support their team members in order to succeed.

Chapter eighteen

Attention to detail

"The difference between something good and something great is the attention to detail." - Charles R. Swindoll

The definition is accomplishing a task through concern to all the areas involved.

Attention to detail requires a combination of soft skills. This includes, active listening, excellent organisation, analytical thinking, time management and observational skills. Focussing on the detail can enable a front-line police officer to spot potential evidence, prevent criminal activity and identify a vehicle or individual linked to a crime.

A skill closely associated with this is personal responsibility. For example, it is vital to ensure that all your kit is in good working order before heading out onto the streets. If you patrol alone and need to search in the darkness and your torch battery has run out, it's not only unprofessional in that you can miss potential evidence at a crime scene, it can also amount to a serious health and safety issue.

We can actively improve our skill area by focussing on one task at a time and eliminate as many distractions as we can. Therefore, when we are completing an important report or maybe even a written statement from a victim of crime, try and use a room that is quiet, well-lit with natural light and airy. Consider turning off mobile devices and personal radios. Active listening is essential when taking a witness statement from a victim and you should demonstrate that you are listening by eye contact and also giving verbal feedback to confirm what the person is asking you to record. If it is a long report or statement, ensure that you take regular breaks to split it into smaller sessions. To ensure attention to detail always 'proofread' documents and communications before signing them off or sending them.

Generally speaking, if you work hard at becoming more organised by paying attention to time management and taking personal responsibility it should enable you to concentrate and focus on the task in hand.

Following my six-month attachment to the crime squad, dealing with drug suppliers and serious crime, the senior management team appointed me for my second spell on the motor vehicle crime squad. There had been an increase of vehicle theft in the Borough, constituting to large proportion of the overall crime statistics.

I was asked to put together a small team to combat the problem. There was no lack of volunteers and I settled for officers who had a proven track record and known to be 'thief takers'.

I had information that there was a group of mainly white youths, who predominantly lived within the Borough, who were actively involved in stealing and 'ringing' cars. They were using lock up garages to work on stolen cars and changing their identity by removing engine and chassis numbers. Sometimes, the youths would respray the vehicles with a different colour and fit parts on from other stolen vehicles. Although it appeared that they were not really benefiting substantially from their criminal

95

activity, they were very active and together as a group, they were pushing the crime figures out of control.

They often used the cars to take part in illegal car gatherings in nearby Romford and Southend and some of the main suspects had been arrested by officers from these areas who had suspected that the cars they were driving were stolen. However, in the majority of cases, no charges were preferred because police had been unable to identity the vehicles' true origin.

Over the following couple of months, we systematically stopped several of the suspects in possession of various cars that we suspected of having their identity changed and seized them. In fact, at one stage we had at least ten of their cars Impounded and under investigation. When the suspects were interviewed, they tended not to incriminate themselves but by using active listening and intelligent questioning, they were happy to talk about the exploits of others. By adopting this tactic, we were able to obtain information about locations of car thefts and sometimes the identity of the owners.

However, the difficulty that we had was that we had a collection of high-powered cars that were not readily identifiable and the information that we had about them was not specific enough. We had to look even closer for other identifying features on the vehicles, such as unique dents, scratches, and window stickers. Our investigation took us to Chalk Farm depot, the base of the MPS stolen car squad. It was here that the details of stolen cars were retained by paper documents that had been completed by the owners when they reported the car stolen to police. They showed specific details of the stolen car and could assist a police officer to identify a vehicle even if the vehicle's index number, chassis and engine numbers had been removed or changed.

The process was painstaking and labour intensive because we had to cross reference the suspected dates and locations of a theft from information that we had obtained from our interviews with suspects and then compare the details on the form with features on the suspected stolen car.

I had a good team and we were able to contact the owners of the cars and arrange for them to attend the car pound, positively identify their car and then provide a detailed written statement from them.

On one occasion, I examined a Ford Sierra that had its identity cleverly changed, after one of the suspects had been stopped and detained. I believed that I may have established the location that it had been stolen from as a result of detailed examination of the forms. Unfortunately, it was impossible for me to find a positive identification from features on the bodywork and I made some enquiries with a man who I believed may be the legal owner. The phone call was more in hope than expectation but he was very helpful and he told me about some peculiarities that were unique to his car. He explained that a few months previously, he had a minor accident in the car and he had to respray a small part of it. He remembered that whilst he was spraying it, a small fly came to rest on the bodywork and he inadvertently sprayed over it. He left it in place, rather than disturbing the paintwork.

After finishing the phone call, I looked carefully at the car and saw that it had been resprayed at the rear and on close examination I saw that there was a fly under the paintwork at the exact position that the owner had mentioned.

This was sufficient for a positive identification and the car thief was charged with theft. Our investigations had to be thorough and to be capable of standing up in court to vigorous defence. When you're dealing with the same group of young people time after time, it becomes like a game of cat and mouse, but we gained the respect of them and to my recollection the encounters that we had with them never became physical.

This shows that front line policing is not all about fast car chases or violent encounters with drunks on a Saturday night duty, but soft skills such as paying attention to detail can also stop criminals in their tracks.

Chapter nineteen

Creativity

"You can't use up creativity. The more you use, the more you have." - *Maya Angelou*

Creativity is defined as the use of the imagination or original ideas to create something.

On first impressions, the general public would not consider the Police to be a creative organisation. Most would associate this soft skill as being most prevalent in the arts and theatre. Musicians write music and lyrics, painters produce beautiful works of art, and actors entertain their audiences with thought provoking performances. However, this skill is used in every area of work and also in an individual's personal life.

In the Policing environment, numerous innovations have been created to prevent crime, detect offences, improve communications with the public and increase officer safety solutions. Advances have been made in detection due to new processes using D.N.A. that can now positively evidence that a suspect has been responsible for a crime.

The use of new technology such as in-car computers being installed in Police vehicles means that now front-line officers have vital information available at their fingertips. Personal body cameras have been rolled out and issued to officers dealing with confrontation, to improve public confidence and provide the best evidence to courts. Police teams have also provided positive work stories directly to the public by means of social media such as twitter and Facebook. These are all examples of recent creativity within the Police but the core law enforcement goal remains the same:- To improve community engagement and public safety – Professionalism and discipline will continue to be a key to success.

Despite these new innovations public confidence in the Police has been damaged due to intentional or accidental lapses in discipline by individuals. Therefore, new ways of increasing public support must be considered.

I truly believe that there are only a small number of cops who bring the service into disrepute and the vast majority are hardworking, honest people trying by innovative methods to make our communities safer.

At the start of 1990, I was selected to run a street duties course where new recruits were familiarised of the layout of the Borough and given the first opportunity to deal with crime and suspects under supervision of senior constables. One of the officers who worked beside me had spent most of his career working and walking the beat in the West End of London. He was a problem solver with an alternative way of thinking things through. We complimented each other's skills and strengths so when I was asked to put together the Neighbourhood Policing Team at Bow at the conclusion of the course, I asked him to join me.

I head-hunted several officers who I had previously worked with on the Home Beat Team and who I had confidence in. On my previous posting, which finished two years before, we had achieved some good results with pro-active community policing, but I wanted to go one step further and try and build a 'brand' with the new team. It was slightly controversial and some officers viewed me as a maverick.

The MPS was trying to develop a corporate image at this time by using people who in my opinion had more interest in improving their own promotion ambitions, than reducing crime and the fear of crime in the community. I now understand that it was a slightly unrealistic approach to build a separate 'brand' in a huge organisation but I had previously worked with officers who had a cynical view of policing and a poor attitude towards the general public and I felt that the people of Bow deserved better than that. I did not want to be like those officers and with my 'leading from the front' approach, I had the respect of the majority of the constables that I worked with.

It is really important to give each other time and provide the opportunity for inspiration and creativity. I gathered the team together and outlined my ideas of the 'brand' that residents, especially young people, could identify with and have confidence in us to do the best job for our neighbourhood. Through collaboration, we had a 'brain-storming' session to bounce ideas off each other and we came up with a fictional character who we named 'Bow Bill.' He was to be our logo and it put a bit of fun into local Policing. We also devised a policing package that encompassed most of our activities including arrest and charge, school visit programmes, community meetings, partnerships with the Council and a project called the 'stop-it' campaign. Behind the idea of the package was accountability, providing a value for money service and to promote public confidence. I knew that officers would buy into it and get a high level of job satisfaction from it.

The initiative attracted a lot of interest from response officers and the general public. Local businesses helped us to produce posters and literature promoting 'Bow Bill' and the policing package. In turn, we organised various local charity events and invited our partner agencies and local people along to participate.

Our school visit programme was very successful and involved children in the process in several ways. We invited parties of school children to the police station where they were able to see activities such as police horses being re-shod in the stables. This was a fascinating sight in the middle of London and often unseen. We also asked children to look out for abandoned cars that were parked in their streets and report back to us. Once they began to trust us, they came back to us on a regular basis with registration numbers and locations that helped us recover several stolen vehicles that had previously been untraced. We also formed a sports club where local children could come and take part in new exciting sports and activities. It was a complete community initiative and we became well-known throughout the Borough for our creativity.

The results of our police work were impressive and our statistics in every area of our work were reviewed monthly and fed back through senior management and community meetings. A senior officer called Chief Inspector Shepherd was on a secondment to the Borough from Essex Police. He was so impressed with the 'package' that he put together a report about our effectiveness in combining innovative ideas, public engagement and pro-active policing to reduce crime. It was clear to him and everyone around us that we really enjoyed what we were doing by making a positive difference in the community.

He was determined to introduce a similar scheme in the Essex Force and invited me to attend Brentwood Police Station and give a presentation to his Sergeants. He addressed his officers saying that at that time that it was the only thing that he had seen in the MPS that really worked. It was a tremendous compliment to me and my team, but looking back at his comments they may have antagonised some senior Met officers who possibly later wanted to reduce the project to mediocrity.

It was a great time for the team and creativity in the police should be looked upon as a good thing, especially where it improves public trust and public confidence.

Looking back at it now maybe we put a bit too much pressure on ourselves and my advice is to ensure that you give yourself a break from time to time, so that you can take your mind off the task and come back to it refreshed and focussed.

Chapter twenty

Bravery

"I learned that courage was not the absence of fear, but the triumph over it. The brave man is not he who does not feel afraid, but he who conquers that fear." - Nelson Mandela

Bravery can be defined as courageous behaviour or character.

Bravery can be seen in people young and old and from all walks of life. It is normally associated with doing heroic acts in highly dangerous or precarious situations but it can also be demonstrated in more ordinary encounters such as a person standing up against unfairness or adversity.

However, my personal experience of meeting a person who had shown extreme bravery was my grandfather, Herbert Harvey. He was a Sergeant in the 7th Hussars in the first world war and was awarded a Distinguished Conduct medal for acts of bravery when on horseback and under fire from the enemy. Only a few awards were given out to 7th Hussars in the Great war so he must have been a courageous man.

I remember him as a tough, but very humble man, who established businesses in Bow in East London. He always respected the Police and enjoyed a drink, in moderation in the nearby Lord Campbell pub.

There are numerous examples of bravery within the police service with officers running into burning buildings, tackling armed offenders, being shot at, stabbed and driven at. Sadly, these acts of bravery sometimes result in tragedy.

There is the case of P.C. Andrew Harper, who in 2019 responded to a report of a burglary near Sulhamstead, Berkshire. Late on in his duty, he came across three teenage males who were driving a car and P.C. Harper ended up being dragged by the car for nearly a mile, thereby causing his death. The youths were arrested and acquitted of murder but found guilty of manslaughter. His wife championed a campaign for a change the law that led to the mandatory sentence for life imprisonment for anyone killing emergency workers.

In August 2019, P.C. Stuart Outten was patrolling in Leyton, East London, when he stopped a man called Muhmmad Rodwan, who was driving a white van. Rodwan attacked the officer using a large machete, inflicting multiple stab wounds and fracturing the officer's skull. Incredibly, P.C. Outten survived the attack and was able to 'taser' Rodwan and detain him. The officer received a National Police bravery award.

More recently P.C. Ryan Curtis and P.C. Scott James were awarded a merit star by Essex Police for their brave action when arresting Ali Harbi Ali, who murdered M.P. Sir David Amess in Leigh on sea, Essex in 2021. The officers were called to the incident where Ali was in wait for them at the scene of the crime with the murder weapon. The officers subdued Ali and arrested him.

These are three examples of quite extreme cases but we can all develop our courage and overcome our fear in our everyday lives by taking small steps out of our comfort zone to improve our self-confidence. We all make mistakes but we must not be afraid of failure. It's important to understand our limits but we have to learn to cope with difficulty so that it becomes a habit.

I never considered myself to be a brave person but the reality is when every Police officer steps onto the street whether on duty or not they are obliged by law to deal with an unknown threat from any potential assailant. The public often forget that Police officers are only human and it is the duty of every citizen to assist a constable if reasonably called on to do so.

In early 1991, I was leading the Bow Neighbourhood team in my second attachment to the home beat officers. Arresting suspects was an everyday part of the job that was made easier because of the familiarity and knowledge that we had of local criminals. Anonymity is the chief weapon against Police for law breakers and when officers are encouraged to work with continuity a lot of the potential violent confrontations can be avoided.

It was a sunny afternoon when I left the Police Station on foot patrol with another officer. We had only walked about 100 yards along Addington Road when I noticed a black youth, who was about 20 years old, loitering near to a stairwell in a block of flats. The footpath we were walking on and the spot where the youth was loitering was separated by metal railings that were about five feet in height. I became suspicious of the youth as he was acting furtively and I had not seen him hanging about the area before.

I walked towards him across a patchy, grassed area and as I approached the youth started to walk away, so I called to him. There are only usually two options if a suspect is confronted in this type of situation and he is guilty of some crime. The first option is to run away and make good his escape and the second is to speak to the officer and try and bluff it out, face to face. The youth, who I will refer to as Josh, took the second option and he approached me. We met face to face on the grassed area and I asked him what he was doing there. He immediately became agitated, turning his head from side to side. When questioned further, he was defensive and started shouting. He was taller than me, he had quite a muscular build and athletic looking. He was wearing heavy clothing. I decided to search him, taking all the circumstances into consideration and when I tried to lay hands on him, I immediately felt his body tense up.

Out of the corner of my eye, I saw that my colleague was leaning on the railings on the other side to where I was trying to search the youth as he had not anticipated that there would be an escalation to the encounter. As I searched the back of the suspects waistband, I found what I immediately recognised as the handle of a large knife. I pulled it out of the waistband and as I did the suspect grabbed hold of my other arm as if to throw me to the floor. I instinctively threw the knife as far as I could to prevent giving the suspect the opportunity of grabbing it and using it on me. Of course, I was off balance and the youth threw me to the ground in a type of judo move.

He ran off and I gathered myself together, got up off the ground and pursued him on foot. Although he was wearing training shoes and he was fast, I was fit and determined. I managed to keep him in sight as he ran through a small tunnel (Called Tom Thumbs Arch) under the main London to Southend railway line and into another council estate.

My colleague was less fit than me, as he was a smoker and slightly over-weight and was left behind on the foot chase. I radioed for assistance as I was on the move and the suspect ran into an entrance block then doubled back out of sight and disappeared from view. I did not know the reason why he was carrying a knife and I didn't know if he was in possession of another weapon that I hadn't been able to find. I just focussed on trying to find him as I knew he couldn't have made an escape from the estate and he must be hiding in the near vicinity. The foot chase had only been over a few hundred yards but it was at 'sprint speed' while I was wearing body armour. I was breathing heavily; I was sweating and disorientated. From when I was first in the Police at Liverpool, I always had a hunter instinct and it was always seen as a bad thing or failure if a prisoner escaped from you. I wanted to detain him and arrest him for carrying the weapon. That was non-negotiable.

A Police car came screaming up to assist me but despite explaining to the two officers inside that the suspect had to be hiding in the very near vicinity, for an unknown reason they sped off in the car to the other side of the estate leaving me on my own in a state of breathlessness. Although I was surprised and a bit confused at the actions of the officers, I continued to search for the suspect. I started to check underneath the parked vehicles on the estate and suddenly I found him, face down under a large van. On seeing me, he started to slide himself out on his belly and for a few moments I thought he was going to give himself up quietly. However, seeing that I was on my own, he launched himself at me and we crashed to the ground with his weight on top of me, falling onto a concrete surface. I felt my left knee 'explode' and I immediately realised that I had been badly injured.

Somehow, I managed to grapple with him and hold him to the floor, whilst at the same time I shouted for urgent assistance over the personal radio. Other officers arrived on scene and the suspect was handcuffed and placed in a Police van. Even as he sat in the van I could visibly see on his face that he was agitated and breathing deeply. I could sense that he was still determined to evade confinement and on the way back to the Police Station he tried to throw himself head first out of the rear doors of the Sherpa van by launching himself at them while the van was moving along a main road. Fortunately, the doors held firm but I would hate to think what might have come of it if he had been successful in forcing them open.

Josh, the suspect, appeared at Magistrates court a few weeks later and was found guilty of possession of a knife and assaulting a police officer. He was fined £100.

Following the altercation, I went to hospital and was examined by a doctor who could not identify any broken bones. However, after having three days sick leave I returned to work where I had to take responsibility for my rehabilitation and take care not to put myself in potentially violent situations for a while. I had constant knee problems resulting from the injury and 30 years later it was necessary for me to have knee replacement surgery.

It was suspected that Josh was 'collecting' money from a drug user at the time of the confrontation but it was never verified.

Chapter twenty-one

Conflict resolution

"All conflicts, no matter how intractable, are capable of peaceful resolution."- Nelson Mandela
The definition of conflict resolution is the process of ending a conflict by co-operating and problem solving.

This skill should be an integral part of a Police officer's toolkit as it's an everyday occurrence where officers have to deal with conflict in the form of people arguing or even making threats towards them or other persons. Its therefore important that officers develop the skills and awareness to de-escalate the conflict, remain calm, and take care not to inflame the situation by their words or behaviour.

Some officers are much more adept at doing this by using a combination of soft skills such as building a rapport with interpersonal communication, displaying empathy, showing patience and actively listening.

It tends to be a much more straightforward process when dealing with a person who is sober and who are willing to listen to reason. It is more complex if an individual or group are intoxicated and as a result may be less willing to listen and are focussed on the argument.

There are times when an officer deals with an incident which requires reasonable force from the outset and it comes with experience that the officer has to take into account all available information and the demeanour of the individuals in front of him. This can be referred to as situation awareness. The officer must consider officer safety issues and conduct early negotiation with the person. Consideration must also be given to allowing space between officer and 'suspect' and be prepared to back off if necessary.

Teamwork is important especially if there is more than one person involved and officers should conduct a dynamic risk assessment around the size and build of the people involved, potential threats such as weapons and the place environment. (People – objects - place)

Sometimes, officers will deal with individuals with communication difficulties such as people with mental health issues or who are not fluent in speaking English. In these situations, it is especially important to be sensitive and compassionate. Try and build a rapport with them with a low consistent voice. Demonstrate that you are not a threat by adopting an open stance and using reassuring body language.

Finally, it's useful to remember how people get locked into a vicious circle of communication based on how their attitudes and behaviour respond to each other. It's referred to as a model called 'Betaris Box'. In short, it shows that 'my attitude' affects 'my behaviour' which affect 'your attitude' which affects 'your behaviour' which affects 'my attitude' and so on. For effective conflict resolution if the officer gets drawn into this circle he or she must try and break it immediately.

1992 was a transitional year for me. I had developed the Bow Neighbourhood team into a tight, effective crime fighting unit and I had been trusted to work, more or less unsupervised, while building strong links with the community. I had 15 years' service at this time and I was used to dealing with conflict situations. It was quite usual to experience resistance from suspects at the time of arrest or at the scene of incidents such as domestic disputes or from groups of youth fighting in the street. I always used my experience to defuse an incident rather than having to resort to force. However, you expect conflict from members of the public but you do not expect to have it from your colleagues in a similar way.

At this time there was a shift around with personnel on the team and a new senior officer was put in charge of us. He came from a Police unit that was not noted for its subtle policing skills because the officers were employed to quell major disorder or public demonstrations. Shortly after his arrival on the team he removed one of my most trusted officers and transferred him to another division. The officer was experiencing major trauma from a family issue at the time and I felt that he had been treated unfairly and no compassion had been shown towards him.

One morning, I had a heated disagreement with the supervisor and to cut a long story short, I was unceremoniously told to go home and I was transferred to Havering division on the outskirts of the M.P.S. Looking back, I could have dealt with the face to face conflict in a better way as it was obvious that a higher ranking officer will always be supported over a subordinate. The manner in which I was dealt with made me resentful and angry. I felt let down because I had given good service to the Borough and had been fully committed to work and building trust with the residents.

I initially started work again as a Sergeant on a response team at Romford Police Station doing routine custody officer and section sergeant duties. These are essential jobs and I have the utmost respect for officers who work on response teams, sometimes all their service. The main role for us was mainly dealing with shoplifters in the day and night club fights on late shifts.

Romford was the main Police Station on the division and after a few months I was posted to Rainham. This was an old Essex Police Station that had been amalgamated into the Met following boundary changes back in 1964. It was located on the old A13 trunk road which at the time was one of the busiest 'A' roads in the U.K. The station was basically a house with no custody facilities and had two police houses adjoining it on each side.

There had been a shake-up in policing and I found myself in charge of a small team of officers on a new type of 'sector' policing initiative. Each team had to work as a response unit on earlies, late turn and night duty but on their downtime officers were expected to perform a community role. I think it was reasonable to say that most officers were sceptical about their new role or were resistant because they were more comfortable with mobile response duties.

I got on well with my team of officers and had the respect of them. I carried on with my job and encouraged my team to be pro-active and get involved in community meetings, school visits and local issues. I was still feeling that I had been badly treated at the end of my time at Tower Hamlets and I tried to avert my feelings by being very pro-active. In fact, in the two years at Rainham I made

114

nearly 300 arrests, the highest number for any individual officer on the Borough. It was very easy to be active in the Rainham area as it had a lot of industrial premises and large residential population. However, it was under-policed. Arrests for theft of cars, burglary and assaults were fairly easy to come by but it did come at a cost of neglecting my supervisory duties.

The teams were small and one night duty I paraded just two male officers and myself. I had a feeling that something had annoyed one of them, who I will refer to as Steve, but I posted the two constables in one vehicle and I intended to drive the other vehicle alone. Just before I went on patrol Steve confronted me about my decision of not letting a female officer, who I will refer to as Sarah, work on a Bank holiday. Traditionally Bank holidays are paid at double time and therefore response teams were run on restricted resources for budget reasons. Steve had been put down to work and I fully explained my decision. Steve exploded into a rage, shouting and verbally abusing me. I had failed to notice that both of them had recently broke up from their respective partners and they had formed a relationship. Steve obviously wanted to work with Sarah and he felt that I was being unfair to her. I stuck to my guns and told him firmly, but politely that my decision stood. He was so enraged that he shouted verbal abuse at me and just when I thought that it could get physical, he stormed out and drove the Police car off at high speed. This behaviour was out of character for Steve, who was a really good pro-active Policeman. Maybe if anything, he had become a bit too comfortable on Havering division and felt that he could challenge supervisory decisions. The teams were small and we relied on each other for support, so it was a concerning moment for me. I felt that although his behaviour had been unacceptable, I did not want to escalate the disagreement and thought it was better to give him time to cool off.

I went out on patrol and sometime later I saw the Police car being driven by Steve coming towards me on a quiet road. It suddenly sped up towards me and it appeared to be driven straight at me. I slowed down and just when I thought that he would crash into me he changed direction at the last minute and he drove off. My instincts told me that he was still upset and that he was smouldering over my decision. He screamed over the radio that he was feeling unwell and that he was going home.

For the next couple of days, Steve was on sick leave and other officers were walking on eggshells because they had obviously heard about the incident and wondered what action I would take against him on his return.

Normally behaviour such as this would have warranted a disciplinary hearing but having recently experienced what I felt was an injustice against me, I adopted a different approach to resolve the conflict.

Steve resumed duties when I was performing custody officer duties at nearby Hornchurch Police station and therefore I couldn't be at Rainham on parade on his return. Hornchurch was a very quiet custody suite and at about midnight Steve called me by phone to talk to me alone. When he came into the room, I did not say anything and just let him do the talking. He was immediately very apologetic as he knew that he had been out of order by shouting at me and behaving in an irresponsible manner a few nights before. I did not need to lecture him as he was well-aware that he had been wrong and the consequences of his words and actions could have been very serious for him. We had a 'man to man' talk and I decided that the best course of action should be to shake hands, put it down to experience and move forward.

Steve was a good man and he had been through a difficult time with his break up, therefore I felt that he deserved a bit of understanding and compassion. After this incident Steve never raised his voice to me and always accepted my decisions. This approach to conflict resolution would not have been seen by many as appropriate in the circumstances but it worked in this instance and ended in a favourable outcome by problem solving and co-operation.

Chapter twenty-two

Empathy and active listening

"Empathy is seeing with the eyes of another, listening with the ears of another, and feeling with the heart of another." - Alfred Adler

I have decided to link these two soft skills together in one chapter because active listening is essential when demonstrating empathy.

Empathy can be defined as the ability to see the world through another person's eyes. Active listening is the practice of preparing to listen, observing what non-verbal and verbal messages are being sent, and then providing feedback to demonstrate attentiveness.

Some people may feel that empathy has nothing to do with police work as law enforcement is an authoritarian and often brutal occupation where officers have to use physical force to prevent crime and arrest suspects. However, police work can also be viewed as dealing with human problems that make life difficult for honest law-abiding people. Police officers have to deal with a range of incidents that involve vulnerable people, victims of crime and people suffering from mental illness. In these situations, it is often necessary for officers to be empathetic and try and understand how the other person is feeling.

To develop this skill the officer must pay attention with active listening, try and minimise any distractions and stay mentally tuned in to the conversation. It's also important to focus on any body language including the tone of a person's voice and changes in the persons demeanour.

I have noticed from my own observations that there is a tendency for some modern officers to deal with certain offenders who commit minor misdemeanours as 'victims of society'. These people include street beggars, street drinkers, rowdy groups of people in public places or even shoplifters. The approach taken by officers may be because of a lack of self-confidence or even that they believe that they are showing empathy. There is a fine line between empathy and sympathy which involves understanding from your own perspective. It is crucial for officers to understand that their principal role is that of a law enforcement officer and not just to act as a type of pseudo-social worker. This may be a controversial opinion, but consideration must always be given to the wider, law abiding, community who are affected by the problems. It can give the impression that police are turning a blind eye to the issues by adopting a sympathetic approach and walking away leaving the lawlessness to carry on.

Remember – if the small issues are not tackled effectively, it creates an environment for the more serious crimes to grow and develop.

Empathy does have a role in police work in many situations, but officers should always focus on their role and for the objective of the task that they are undertaking at the time.

I was born in Rainham and working there as a police officer was an enjoyable experience. I knew many of the people who lived there, and I was familiar with the roads and local environment. By this time of my police service, I had experienced dealing with many traumatic and emotional incidents involving the public. Dealing with sudden deaths and delivering death messages required a combination of professionalism, compassion and empathy. I had to use these skills to the full at various incidents during my time at Rainham.

I remember coming on duty one Saturday afternoon when a message came through from Wiltshire Police. It was written in a slightly cryptic way, but the gist of the content was that there had been a traffic accident involving the driver of a car and an army vehicle. The car had caught on fire and the driver, who was believed to be a young female, had been trapped and sadly died. The vehicle had been burnt out and there was difficulty establishing the true identity of the driver. Wiltshire Police asked us to make some enquiries at the home address of the registered keeper.

I went there with an experienced and well-respected constable, called Charlie. By coincidence, when we arrived at the house, I realised that a district nurse who used to come to our house in the past to treat my grandmother in her last years lived there. The nurse was a middle-aged woman of West Indian origin and from memory was a very family orientated person. I imagined what impact that the bad news would have on her if the deceased was in fact her nearest and dearest.

We knocked on the door of the neat semi-detached house and it was answered by the nurse who I immediately recognised and who I will refer to as 'Florrie'. I saw the shock and fear on her face at the sight of two uniformed police officers on her doorstep. Probably from the expressions on our faces she processed that we were there to deliver bad news and she started to scream, "No, no, no." There were two other younger females in the house and we managed to establish that the deceased was in fact Florrie's daughter, who had been a talented singer and had been performing in the Swindon area, the previous night.

The three women became extremely upset and animated. They were screaming and falling to the floor with emotion. They were grabbing hold of me and literally hanging onto my face, not with aggression, but as if to check that I was real and that the whole situation was not a dream. I could only imagine the emotions that they were going through.

After about half an hour of reassuring them, calming them down and empathising with them, we managed to find details of Florrie's son who we spoke to on the telephone. He lived nearby and he arrived at the house after a few minutes. He was naturally distraught, but after a short while, we explained to him that we needed him to keep strong as someone from the family had to take charge and contact the coroner's officer. We stayed for about two hours until everyone had accepted the awful reality. We were professional and respectful to the family throughout.

Sometime later, I met Florrie and I had a conversation with her. She had come to terms with her daughter's untimely death and she thanked me and Charlie for the compassion and empathy that we showed that day.

I had several similar death messages to deliver around this time and there is no doubt that despite remaining professional, the experiences and emotions remain with you and can touch your own life.

Chapter twenty-three

Work life balance

"Strive not to be a success, but rather to be of value." - *Albert Einstein*

The definition is the division of one's time and focus between working and family or leisure activities.

For the first part of my police service there was an expectation that all officers would dedicate their working life, including their off-duty time to police work. There were high disciplinary and professional standards with many older officers coming from a military background. There were fewer female officers in front line roles than now which led to a masculine environment and an unforgiving attitude if a person 'couldn't hack it.'

Officers had to obtain permission from senior officers as to, where they could live, who they could marry and had to provide full contact details of where you would be whilst on annual leave, just in case you were needed back at the station for some unforeseen issue. This often led to some officers writing comments on annual leave forms such as 'touring Cornwall in a camper van.' to avoid being called back. These were in the days before the availability of mobile phones.

The job involved long and unsociable hours working at demonstrations and processing prisoners. It was common practice to attend court hearings off a night duty which would involve finishing work at 6am, maybe catching an hour sleep, before returning to give evidence at court at a morning session.

There was a culture of heavy drinking, especially amongst detectives. In addition to this, officers often failed to have regular meal breaks and in turn it led to a diet of unhealthy take-away meals. As you can imagine all these factors together resulted in many officers suffering from high stress, poor health and problems in their personal lives.

Since these days, there has been more emphasis on creating a balance between work and home life with more support in the form of counselling. Nowadays, with changes to legislation and more women becoming front line officers, there has been an introduction of part time work and even remote working to accommodate modern life.

To avoid burning out, its essential that officers schedule quality time off to reduce the feeling that work is all-consuming and all-powerful. It makes good sense to undertake basic preventative measures including practising physical activity several times a week, getting enough sleep and eating healthily. When on inside duty, it's also important to take breaks during the day, have a short walk or even do some breathing exercises. It's especially necessary if you have been glued to a computer. The key to being more productive at your job is to be aware of the balance between work and your personal life.

After spending two years at Rainham, a memo came round saying that Havering division had too many sergeants and that they were looking for volunteers to move to Hackney and Stoke Newington Police Stations, who were under-staffed. The request was received by horror from most as it became apparent that if there were insufficient volunteers there would be compulsory transfers. I volunteered to move Stations as I saw it as an opportunity to go back to an inner-city area while most sergeants looked at Havering as an easy and convenient posting and refused to go without a fight.

I started at Hackney Police Station in 1994, working again as a response team Sergeant. It was a very different environment from Rainham. The 'nick' was an old building, originating from the early 1900s, with a large back yard and it was adjacent to St. Johns Churchyard off Lower Clapton Road. The officers were generally very pro-active and stuck together through thick and thin. I kept myself busy as usual patrolling and making arrests while combining this with regular custody officer duties.

The Borough was a difficult place to police because there had been several controversial incidents that had attracted media attention where officers had been found to be at fault. The Borough had a very ethnically diverse population and a violent crime and drug problem. Nearly every day there were confrontational incidents with the public who alleged racist behaviour or corrupt practices against officers.

At this time, my own personal life was approaching a crisis and I did not realise that my own stress levels were increasing and I began to suffer from anxiety. This anxiety manifested itself into everyday problems with public speaking and confusion. I struggled to complete the basic tasks such as verbally briefing officers. Despite this, I was head-hunted to set up and lead a new community safety unit. This unit comprised of a racial incident team, a domestic violence unit, crime prevention officers and licensing. It was a complex team to set up because the roles of the various officers were so different and demanding. On reflection, I should not have accepted this role because I was not in the right frame of mind to do an effective job.

It was not long before people started to realise that I was struggling both professionally and personally. I was staying at work until late and I was drinking too much. This came to the attention of a Superintendent in charge and I eventually admitted that my marriage was over and I was suffering from the effects of anxiety. It was difficult to admit these things but I hate to think what might have happened if I hadn't done so.

I look back at it now as not being 'my finest hour' but fortunately the Superintendent was understanding and sympathetic with my situation and allowed me to take time off and recuperate.

Chapter twenty-four

Mental strength

"I survived because the fire inside me burned brighter than the fire around me." - Joshua Graham

Mental strength or toughness can be defined as a measure of individual resilience or confidence that might predict success in sport, education and the workplace.

I have already addressed the subject of resilience and how one can deal with adversity and challenging situations, so in this chapter I am looking at the return of a person recovering from what most people would refer to as a breakdown.

In my case I suffered from anxiety which is a debilitating condition that can be treated as a mental illness. It was explained to me by a doctor that it had manifested itself over time as a result of various personal difficulties and stresses, gradually building up and not being dealt with. The doctor told me that it was similar to gradually filling up a glass of water. While the water hadn't filled the glass I could cope, but if problems escalate and the water continues to fill the glass it will eventually overflow and when that occurs a breakdown can result.

Most people experience a physical reaction such as 'panic attacks' in this situation such as feeling breathless, having an increased heartbeat and feeling 'spaced out' or dizzy. When this occurs the person experiences 'Fight or flight' which is an automatic physiological reaction to an event that is perceived to be stressful or frightening.

There are several ways that health professionals advise people to cope with these attacks and are useful in an ideal world. However, as a front-line police officer it can be difficult to manage the condition, without looking weak or vulnerable.

Nevertheless, it is worth adopting the advice as a routine part of your life. Try and take care of your physical health and put a limit on the amount of alcohol and caffeine that you intake. If you take regular exercise such as walking, jogging, cycling or swimming you will get a feeling of well-being which is good for your mental health. Try and focus on one thing at a time and remember to eat healthily and take regular breaks. Everyone can experience stressful events in life and sometimes we can feel out of control. Make sure that if you feel like this don't be afraid to ask for help from someone who you can talk to and trust.

I returned to work after a break and I had undergone six sessions of counselling from a Met Police counsellor. I suppose the sessions helped me as it was an opportunity to reflect and look to the future. I was in the process of divorce proceedings and I had also lost my house and in my own mind I had lost my self-respect. I was anxious about starting back at Hackney again primarily because I did not know how my colleagues would react to me. I had low self-esteem, a lack of confidence and in my mind I felt like I was a failure.

I started back at work on a response team and I was surprisingly well received by my fellow officers. Of course, I knew that they were aware of my personal circumstances as there are very few secrets that you can keep to yourself in the Police. I would say now that the remainder of my posting to 'G' division was the most challenging time of my career. I look back at it as if I was recovering and surviving but somehow it did not really affect me being an effective Sergeant on the response teams, beat crimes unit and as Criminal Justice Sergeant as I learned to manage the situations and demonstrate mental strength.

I have condensed this period from 1996 to 2002 into one chapter. The reason for this is that I had lost my 'mojo' and my main focus was to deal with my anxiety and put strategies in place to cope. My strategy was to ease myself back into the working environment and try to avoid as many situations as possible that would trigger a reaction. I volunteered for a 6-month posting at City Road Police Station working Monday to Friday on late turn as a custody officer. This may be surprising to some people as this environment can be high pressure and stressful but as I was experienced and confident in the role. I was working on my own and gradually I got back into the groove, improved my self-confidence and felt that I was being really useful. I found that by doing regular duties I had more time for myself in my downtime and more control over my life.

At the conclusion of this posting, I applied to be the Sergeant in charge of the Beat crimes unit, which involved working with and supervising three constables in plain clothes at Stoke Newington Police Station. 'Stokie' had a notorious reputation as some years before a young black man casually walked into the foyer of the Police Station, produced a shotgun, shot himself and died. The locals suspected foul play by Police and these suspicions and a lack of trust led to a tense atmosphere in the area. A new, more 'open plan' police station was constructed following the shooting. For my officers, the posting was a stepping stone to becoming a detective. They were young and enthusiastic even though the role was routine. We had to deal with a high volume of routine, minor crimes such as criminal damage, theft and assault on a daily basis. I recognised that I was now supervising a more modern type of Police officer on the eve of the Millennium. They were better educated and less judgemental than older officers. They were willing to accept change more readily and were comfortable with new technology. They were also very accepting of me although I was a lot older than them but they were also willing to learn from me as they recognised that I had many years of experience in the job.

The majority of victims of minor crime often did not want to appear at court or even make a written statement and therefore it was more of a case of negotiating the best outcomes and managing expectations. Maybe once every week or so we would go out and arrest a suspect when there was sufficient evidence available and we had credible witnesses to a crime. I learnt to delegate more work to the younger officers who were willing and eager to learn, which was part of my coping strategy.

My last posting at 'G' division at Stoke Newington Police Station was that of Criminal Justice Unit Sergeant, where I was responsible for reviewing case papers, liaising with the Crown Prosecution service and officers in charge of cases, and attending court for hearings. I was working regular office hours in a comfortable working environment. But in

2002 I reached the stage where I wanted to move onto a more demanding front line role and complete my recovery.

Chapter twenty-five

Customer Service

"I learned that people will forget what you said, people will forget what you did, but people will never forget how you made them feel."- Maya Angelou

A definition of customer service is the assistance and advice provided by a company to those people who buy or use its products or services.

Over recent years the police force has been re-branded as a service. Years ago, the public would normally contact the police by two methods. They would walk into the front office of a Police station and speak to a police officer, normally a Sergeant in uniform, or make a phone call to the station to report an incident or crime.

It was quite an intimidating experience for most people because they were talking directly to a police officer who in turn would often communicate in an uncompromising and abrupt manner. I remember that many Sergeants adopted this method so that the public would leave the front desk as quickly as possible. Order was always maintained there and any person who came in and caused a disturbance would usually end up in the cells.

As years moved on, more ways of communicating with the police became available. Nowadays, most people carry mobile phones capable of many functions such as emails, text messages, video and photos. It has become a lot easier in theory to contact police. It stands to reason that there has been an increase in contact from the public by mobile devices and digital methods rather than face to face encounters at the Police station.

Strategies and policies have been adopted to cope with this increased demand and there has been an investment by employing civilian workers to improve customer service at help-desks or contact centres. Although this plan may have had some positive benefits it has resulted in police officers becoming more distant from the public. Now, due to a lack of resources, the public only tend to come into contact with police in confrontational situations or if they are a victim or witness to a crime. Unformed officers are rarely seen patrolling on foot, directing traffic or assisting parents and children by doing a school crossing patrol.

It can be a busy and often chaotic life for a response officer who often does not have the time to engage in pleasantries or polite conversation. However, good customer service is essential for a front-line officer in order to be helpful and improve public confidence. It's important to remember that a satisfied customer will tell 3-5 people of their experience while a dissatisfied customer will tell 15-20 people. Therefore, it's important that officers show empathy by imagining what it's like to walk in the other persons shoes. The person may be experiencing stress and it is necessary to actively listen and show some patience. The officer must understand the person's needs, be firm but approachable and importantly, manage the persons expectations at an early stage. The officer should also be careful with the effects of his/her words on the other person. Being able to deliver good customer service can reduce complaints and improve people's perception of the police.

I saw an opportunity to go full circle and return to Tower Hamlets Borough. It was for a position of a uniformed Sergeant to set up and run a new unit called the Prisoner Processing Team (P.P.T.) at Bethnal Green Police Station. It wasn't exactly the front-line policing role that I was looking for but I was enthused by the thought of managing a team again and setting up new processes and systems in order to deal with active cases.

I was given a free rein to bring in officers, work out their duties and brief them. I was aware that the majority of cases would involve prisoners who had been arrested for fairly minor offences such as drug possession, vehicle crime, theft and criminal damage and then left for us to complete the investigation in order that front line officers could return to their duties promptly.

Some of my officers were again grasping the opportunity as a stepping stone to the C.I.D. while others were 'using' it as a break from shift work. I did my utmost to put together processes that were simple and straightforward that allowed us to time manage by making use of cautions and fixed penalty notices as case disposal options.

Customer service was at the heart of the role as we had to routinely deal with victims of crime, witnesses and arresting officers. So it was always necessary to manage their expectations of an outcome at an early stage and make them feel and acknowledge that they had achieved a successful outcome.

On occasions, it was necessary to negotiate with C.I.D. officers who were trying to pass off a case to us that was outside our remit. For example, when a suspect had been arrested for attempted burglary where they had been seen kicking at a door of a building they would try and downgrade the case to an offence of criminal damage so that we would have to take it on. Sometimes, it worked for them, other times we made them investigate what was rightly their case.

Most cases were straightforward and just involved a quick interview of the suspect on tape and caution but there were others that required a more thorough investigation and searches of property under Section 18(1) of PACE.

I remember going on one such search to a council flat in Poplar. A suspect had been found in possession of drugs and from information that we had received we suspected that he may be a 'dealer' with more illegal substances at his home address. I went there with one of my team who was also a 'test purchaser' - a police officer who obtained evidence of drug dealing by posing as a customer in the street. - The officer was very enthusiastic and looked for places in the flat where the suspect may have secreted drugs. He was crawling on the floor of a bedroom when I had to advise him to take care, as I remembered that some years before I had been doing the same at an address in Mostyn Grove in Bow and 'needle-pricked' myself on a discarded hypodermic syringe that was embedded in the carpet. I had a worrying few days afterwards waiting for blood test results which luckily proved to be negative. However, he found a stash of class 'A' drugs and a firearm, which led to a good result with the suspect being charged with multiple offences.

Some of the others were enthusiastic to go the extra mile and I was keen to pass on my experience of dealing with Police informants. It was not unusual for us to identify an active motor vehicle thief or even a burglar and convince them that it would be in their interest for them to confess not only to the crime that they had been arrested for but also to previous offences that they had committed but had not been held to account for. These were referred to as clear-ups or T.I.C.s (Offences taken into consideration). After we had obtained a confession to one of these offences, we would naturally contact the victim who were often impressed that someone had been caught and held accountable for the crime, even if it was not going to be a substantive charge.

I spent the best part of two years running the unit and some of the officers went on to become detectives or progressed their careers by using their experience that they had gained on the team.

Chapter twenty-six

Integrity

"Well you can't trust a special like the old time coppers when you can't find your way home." - Fred W. Leigh and Charles Collins

These were lines from a 1919 Music hall song, 'Don't dilly dally on the way.' made popular by singer Marie Lloyd. It tells a humorous story of a husband and wife doing a 'moonlight flit' after being unable to pay their rent on their lodgings. The wife later stops off at a pub on her own and gets drunk. She reflects that she would be ill advised to approach a volunteer policeman for assistance (a special) as they were thought of as less trustworthy than a regular constable (a copper). It's funny how attitudes involving integrity appear to have changed over the years towards professional police officers despite that the fact that the police are more accountable than ever.

Integrity is the foundation of public service and as I write this even the Prime Ministers' honesty is being called into question following the explanation that he gave to Parliament over the 'Partygate' scandal in Downing Street during the Covid 19 lock-down. It's easy to see how the public can lose trust and confidence in a person who they believe is not being transparent and completely truthful.

There have been several 'high profile' cases reported in the media that have resulted in damaging public confidence in the police. The case of Wayne Cousins, a serving Metropolitan Police officer, who abused his authority and murdered Sarah Everard was chilling. He illegally arrested Sarah, handcuffed her, raped and strangled her, before burning her body and disposing of her remains. He was sentenced to life imprisonment.

In another case, an investigation was conducted into harassment and racism in a unit at Charing Cross Police Station. Examination of a social media group revealed evidence of misogyny, discrimination and sexual harassment amongst officers. In a third case, two Police officers were jailed following the sharing of photographs that they took and shared to others on their phone of two murdered sisters while they were guarding a crime scene in Wembley.

I would like to think of these incidents as being isolated within the Police and that these 'bad apples' are rooted out and dealt with, taking into account that the MPS alone has over 30,000 Police officers. It again demonstrates that unprofessional behaviour and criminal behaviour can severely damage the reputation of an organisation.

So what is integrity? The definition is the quality of being honest and having strong moral principles.

It is about always doing the right thing even when the choice is not easy. It's about the choice we make and keep making every moment of our lives. If you listen to your heart and speak the truth, life becomes easy. It is an essential quality for a Police officer and is non-negotiable. Therefore, when appointing a police officer to the service every effort should be made to check his/her background.

You can develop or preserve your integrity by firstly, clearly define your values. In other words, values that you will never compromise. Secondly, you should know what is right and what is wrong and make every effort to adopt the right choices. You should ask yourself the question, "Will I feel okay with myself?" - before making the choice. Thirdly, develop friendships and work relationships with people who have integrity. They are often people who are humble and self-confident. Try and take responsibility for your actions and don't make promises that you know you can't keep.

In 2004, after completing two years in the prisoner processing team at Bethnal Green Police Station and leaving the unit operating efficiently, I was asked by a senior officer if I would be interested in becoming a Sergeant in charge of one of the new Safer Neighbourhood Teams (SNT's). I had 27 years Police service and the teams were introduced as part of a larger programme to promote community safety.

The purpose was for Police and partner agencies to work together with local communities to identify issues of local concern such as tackling anti-social behaviour, graffiti, disorder and quality of life issues. I was assigned to be in charge of the Shadwell ward team in Tower Hamlets, which was only the second team to be put in place on the Borough. Shadwell was home to a large population of south Asian Muslims and also had the unenviable reputation of having the highest number of disturbance calls from the public in the MPS area at this time.

On my first day there, I was asked to attend a residents meeting on the Glamis estate. I had experience of dealing with people in community meetings from my days at Bow and Rainham, so I was undaunted by having to go there.

These meetings are often sparsely attended but to my surprise, on this occasion, I walked into a community hall packed with residents. The meeting was chaired by a woman called Mary who was known to be formidable and would not hold back from being critical of Police. The residents were loud and clearly passionate about restoring order on their estate.

As the meeting progressed it became apparent that the residents were being intimidated by a gang of youths of Bangladeshi origin who did not live on the estate but spent most of their time hanging around in Cable Street or the nearby Martineau estate. The residents had been let down by successive beat officers who had promised solutions but had delivered very little in the way of tangible results.

As I spoke about my intention of resolving the problems the residents were shouting in frustration that they had heard it all before from other Police officers. Despite only having two other inexperienced constables on the team, I believed that as we were dedicated to the area, we could sort out some of the deep-rooted disorder problems that existed there. I therefore decided to make a promise to residents that if they did not visibly notice an improvement in police action by the next meeting in three months, I would stand down. The residents were impressed by this commitment but sceptical at my statement, however, they went home in a more hopeful mood.

Within a few days we went about patrolling the area in uniform and working to a simple but well-practised strategy. We were able to gather evidence of anti-social behaviour against perpetrators by using our powers under the Police Reform Act 2002 and build cases against for anti-social behaviour court orders. (ASBO's) under the Crime and Disorder Act 1998.

This positive action attracted a considerable amount of media attention and a journalist called Robert Hardman from the Daily Mail came to interview me. He walked the streets with me and met local residents. He subsequently wrote a full spread article in the newspaper entitled 'Dixon of Drug Green', comparing me with the fictional character 'Dixon of Dock Green.'

At the next residents meeting I had a much easier time because I had been true to my word and demonstrated integrity and fulfilling my promise. Residents had seen us patrolling in uniform every day and arresting the main suspects involved in the disturbances.

This was a first step to success in the SNT but there were still many challenges to come.

Chapter twenty-seven

Public speaking

"It usually takes more than three weeks to prepare a good impromptu speech." - Mark Twain

Public speaking also called oratory or oration has traditionally meant the art of speaking face to face with a live audience.

It is essential as a police officer to learn the techniques of public speaking as they will often be called to speak on a public stage, whether giving evidence at court, delivering a briefing to colleagues or taking part in a presentation or meeting. Of course, not everyone can make a speech without practice but there are certain skills that can be learnt to make a speech effective and even entertaining. As a novice it is worth reading the words of famous speeches or even listening to recordings of them. The following are good examples of notable and well-known speeches.

In May and June 1940, Sir Winston Churchill made three memorable speeches during the period of the battle of France in the second world war. The first was on 13th May and is referred to as the 'Blood, toil, tears and sweat' speech. The second was 'We will fight them on the beaches' was delivered on 4th June. The third was 'This was their finest hour' speech on 18th June. Churchill delivered these speeches to Parliament at a time of great adversity but by using his oratory skills, he was able to inspire the nation with his 'never give in' attitude.

In 1963, Martin Luther King junior, a Baptist minister and American civil rights activist delivered a speech during the march on Washington for jobs and freedom. It is referred to as 'I have a dream' speech calling for civil and economic rights and an end to racism. He spoke with feeling and hope for the future and it is looked upon as one of the most iconic speeches in American history.

More recently, Barack Obama gave a speech at the 2004 Democratic convention known as the 'Audacity of hope' speech. It was about reclaiming the American dream. He delivered it in a thoughtful, slow and decisive manner which propelled him to national prominence prior to his election as President of the United States.

A police officer may not be capable of delivering such memorable speeches but can develop the basics of public speaking and should always be aiming to improve. If you observe Obama he delivers a speech in a slow and measured way, taking time to pause and breathe. If you are nervous before speaking to an audience, it is best to use notes but not read from them verbatim as it may not appear that the words have integrity. This is important when giving evidence at court. It is also essential that the speaker must 'know their audience' and prepare and practice the speech accordingly. Visual aids, such as a power-point presentation, can be useful especially if the speaker is suffering from nerves as the focus can be moved from the speaker to the slide-show and vice-versa. However, the most necessary advice to an orator giving a speech is to speak the truth.

BY 2005, the Safer Neighbourhood Programme was well under way and as we were one of the first teams to come on line we were producing some excellent outcomes from our patrolling and partnership efforts. The area in and around Watney Street, in Shadwell (which is only a stone's throw from the infamous Siege of Sidney Street in January 1911) had a high incidence of illegal drug use and rough sleeping. We worked hard to reduce the problem by making arrests for possession of drugs, building cases for anti-social behaviour orders and collaborating with the Council to deal with graffiti and homelessness issues.

On 10th March 2005, nearly 28 years into my service, I was asked to speak at the official Safer Neighbourhoods launch at the Ecology Pavilion in Mile End. Rumour had it that certain senior officers did not wish to speak because the event was being attended by the Met. Commissioner, Sir Ian Blair together with M.P.'s and other local dignitaries.

I decided to prepare the speech together with a visual power-point presentation, truthfully demonstrating the impact that pro-active community policing could have on the environment by working closely with partner agencies.

I used our problem-solving model around Watney Market as our example as it was a recent success that could easily be evidenced. On the day, I rehearsed the speech in the morning of the event, checking the duration of it and also ensuring that the presentation equipment was working properly.

I confess that I had nerves on the day, presenting to 150 people in attendance but I delivered it in a slow but meaningful way that brought approval from the attentive audience. Sir Ian Blair handed me his speech notes after the event and I still have them to remind me of the day.

He was a great supporter of good Neighbourhood policing and he returned on more than one occasion to speak to me and my team to ask for feedback about progress of the programme.

Chapter twenty-eight

Problem solving

"Every problem has a solution, it may sometimes just need another perspective." - Katherine Russell

Problem solving is the process of finding solutions to difficult or complex issues. Solving crime and disorder has always been about problem solving but in the past it was deemed unnecessary to record planning or decision making during policing operations.

Recently, processes have been developed to train front line officers and to encourage them to adopt a consistent approach to the problem solving process (P.S.P.) The processes are there to reduce:-

1. Crime and disorder
2. The fear of crime
3. Road traffic collisions
4. Calls for service

During my time as a SNT Sergeant there was a drive to train all officers in the process and encourage them to record all actions. There is a system referred to by an acronym 'SARA' that has four parts.

1. **S**canning – the identification of a specific problem
2. **A**nalysis – Thorough analysis to understand the problem
3. **R**esponse – Development of a tailored response
4. **A**ssessment – Of the effects of the response

The process was quite new to many police officers as in their previous roles they usually worked on their own initiative and rarely became involved with partner agencies in the process of crime reduction. Therefore, officers had to develop new skills to work in collaboration with others. Police officers had to develop good organisation and communication in order to bring the relevant agencies together and effectively chair meetings to deal with the problem itself.

Police had to become accustomed to being transparent and be open to new ideas and possible solutions. It was essential that partners felt that they were being listened to and were involved in the process, so that they would return back to future meetings with the outcomes of any actions they had been allocated. I found that quite often partner agencies are not as quick to complete actions as police and had to be reminded about the importance of their response. Generally speaking, the result of any P.S.P. was due to good communication between Police and partner agencies and publicising the achievements by social media and newspaper articles.

When I first arrived at Shadwell, the analysis revealed that the main causes of concern were youth disorder, reckless driving and illegal drug dealing in the street. The problems were particularly evident in the area of Watney Street around the junction of Cable Street. The area was locally known as 'the front line'. Within a radius of 100 yards there was a Docklands Light railway station, an underground interchange station on the East London line, several shops, a public house and plenty of space for youths to loiter in gangs and to intimidate passers-by.

Looking at it for a period of time, youths would drive up at speed in cars without consideration for pedestrians. There were often fights in the street amongst youths over priority for drug dealing. It was a very intimidating environment for commuters and especially single women who often suffered verbal abuse from the young males.

We had already made a significant difference by reducing crime in the Watney Market area and on the Glamis and Martineau estates, but it was quite clear that this area posed a more difficult problem to work through and provide a solution.

I already had a strategy in mind when I assembled a problem-solving group consisting of a number of partner agencies. When I outlined my proposed objectives for the P.S.P. area some of them were understandably sceptical because the problem was deep-rooted and historic. It was apparent to me that the issues could not just be solved by intensive policing alone and that physical changes would have to be made to the street environment.

We adopted an **evidenced-based approach** and we identified the most active criminal suspects with the intention of using the best information that we could get and using all the ASB tools available to us. We adopted an unofficial zero tolerance policy with people found in possession of illegal drugs and good simple policing tactics such as 'stop and search' produced impressive results. We built strong cases against suspects for anti-social behaviour orders and we also made a few 'high profile' arrests on drug dealers who received custodial sentences.

These interventions were not only effective in that persons were arrested and charged but it sent out a clear message that we were not going to tolerate open drug use or dealing. Our targets who were made subject of an ASBO had strict conditions placed on them not to enter the 'front line' area or to associate with named persons. This seriously affected their ability to deal in the street.

One of our chosen partners was a traffic police officer who was influential with getting the council to change the street environment. Despite the council at first being against our recommendations for change, he was able to convince them that they should extend the controlled area of a zebra crossing in Watney Street, outside the DLR station. They also erected railings on the pavement to prevent Jay walking. These simple measures prevented youths parking their cars in the street and hanging about in their familiar spots. There was a sense of order restored to the area.

When we were off duty one evening, there was a disturbance in the street involving local youths and two white men. There wasn't a crime report on it but we found out about it because we checked the overnight '999' call list. We immediately requested that the council check the street CCTV for the area and sure enough, the incident had been fully captured by the cameras. We were able to identify one of the youths from the images and we made an arrest for affray. This demonstrated that we would fully investigate any incident that came to our notice and take action against offenders.

We had set ourselves a time frame for the process. With the help of council officers, working together with our Police community support officers we were able to evaluate its success from surveys and examining the reduction in Police demand using statistics.

We held a final meeting with our partners and then it was a case of monitoring the area with our patrol strategy to ensure that similar problems did not re-surface. It was a very satisfying result and everyone involved in the problem-solving group played their part in its success.

Chapter twenty-nine

Building trust

"You build trust with others each time you chose integrity over image, truth over convenience, or honour over personal gain." - John C. Maxwell

Trust is the firm belief in the reliability, truth or ability of someone or something.

Police officers have a responsibility to build and develop trust and confidence with the community. In the U.K. we have a long-standing philosophy of policing by consent and the principle dates back to when the Metropolitan Police was formed in 1829.

Robert Peel set out nine principles in policing and were issued in 'General Instructions'. In short, he outlined that it was important to prevent crime and disorder with the cooperation and the approval of the public and to use physical force only when necessary. The test of police proficiency was the absence of crime and not the visible evidence of police action in dealing with them.

The police have not always been popular and at times have encountered resistance from various communities about the means they have dealt with certain issues and problems. Recent history has shown that the handling of a single incident has the potential of damaging trust in the police and can lead to serious disorder if communication lines are not promptly put in place to explain police action.

Sometimes, a solitary officer can be responsible such as in the cases of 'the murder of George Floyd' in the United

States and the 'murder of Sarah Everard' in the U.K. by a rogue MPS officer.

On other occasions, it can be the perceived failure to investigate offences effectively as in the case of the murder of Stephen Lawrence in 1993, where the MPS were subsequently labelled as 'institutionally racist'. It is apparent that the message to build trust with communities must come from the top and any inappropriate behaviour by police should be addressed firmly and promptly.

It is not unusual for a response officer to spend the whole of a shift just dealing with conflict situations but it should be stressed that every contact with the public must be conducted in a professional manner and any mistakes should be admitted and early apologies given to a victim. Even response officers should be encouraged to engage with the public when parked up or on a short patrol.

School visits by Police are a great opportunity to develop contacts and build trust. It is recommended that officers who are selected for this activity are properly prepared so that they can engage with teachers, parents and children. Similarly, officers should be encouraged to attend public events such as summer fetes or concerts on duty where their priority is focussed on reassurance rather than enforcement. Officers who are skilled at I.T. can be useful to send out positive messages on social media but care should be taken when publishing the content and the use of particular words within the message that could be viewed as being controversial.

Some officers are naturally more adept with the use of soft skills than others and it must be recognised that integrity and continuity are essential qualities to ensure that trust is maintained.

I had one more year to serve in the police. For the previous two years I had been working with my Shadwell team, supporting the law-abiding community, building trust and always being prepared to be held accountable by residents. We organised periodic ward meetings where local residents could attend and air their concerns and receive feedback about crime trends. We ensured that we were visible at local events and we developed a network of partners that we could rely on to provide us with information and act as an 'early warning system' for emerging problems.

Despite all these initiatives, we could not be on duty 24/7 and there were naturally times when things came to our attention retrospectively.

One day, I was summoned to attend a public meeting at our base at St. Georges Town Hall in Cable Street by a Superintendent. My team had been on rest days over the weekend and we had not been informed of any unusual occurrence while we had been away. The Superintendent was a very inspiring leader, who was very community minded and knew the value of good neighbourhood policing. He briefed me prior to the meeting that a serious incident had taken place on the ward the previous day that caused considerable community tension.

Shadwell had a historic reputation of conflict between white youths and Asian males. The youths from the Bangladeshi background were generally much smaller in stature than their white counterparts and banded themselves together in numbers for reasons of protection. In 2006, such incidents were relatively uncommon but there had been some resurgence with a right-wing group called the EDL (English Defence League) becoming more vocal and confrontational. However, on this occasion a group of white football supporters randomly got off a train at Shadwell, caused a disturbance and beat up a youth of Bangladeshi origin. A group of his friends pursued the white men and subsequently assaulted one of them quite seriously. Police were called to the scene, including the duty Inspector and arrested some of the local youths on suspicion and took them into custody. None of the white men were arrested and there was a general feeling amongst the community that police had acted in a heavy handed and one-sided manner.

The meeting itself was attended by a cross section of residents including several local youths. Initially the meeting was loud and vociferous towards me and the Superintendent but after about a quarter of an hour we were able to engage in constructive dialogue and explained what we knew about the details of the incident. We conveyed to them that the police may not have had the full facts at the time of making the arrests, as it had been difficult to gather all the evidence in a highly charged atmosphere. We emphasised that sometimes mistakes are made but two wrongs do not make a right. We pointed out that police could have been alerted before the situation had escalated and the retribution handed out to the suspected perpetrators.

I became aware of two men in the audience who were quite obviously activists, who did not appear to represent the community and were merely searching for an opportunity to criticise the police, stir up bad feeling and increase community tension.

However, I was a local officer and was able to connect with the youths and reassure them that a full investigation would be conducted into the matter and it would be the C.P.S. who would be responsible for any charging decisions when all the facts were known.

The youths trusted me as an honest officer with a firm but fair approach. The Superintendent's presence as a senior Police officer also reassured them that the matter would be taken seriously and that we would carry through our promise. Because of these factors the audience were satisfied they had been listened to and they trusted that their friends would get a fair hearing from the Police. I noticed that the activists who had attended the meeting left without the support of the community.

There are many benefits from building trust with residents and having an officer who provides continuity to local policing. This was a case where early intervention, together with effective dialogue worked in our favour to reduce community tension.

Chapter thirty

Patience

"Patience is not the ability to wait, but the ability to keep a good attitude while waiting." - unknown

One final soft skill that a police officer must learn is patience. The definition of which is the capacity to accept or tolerate delay, problems or suffering without becoming annoyed or anxious.

Nowadays, we are living in a world where everything is instant. We expect fast delivery of food, immediate communication by mobile and email and instant credit. It's no wonder that many of us have forgotten what it means to be patient. Before the digital age people had to plan and budget for family meals, use coin-operated telephone boxes, write letters to communicate with friends and save up their money to buy household items. Many of us become anxious in the modern world over situations that require us merely to step back and accept that sometimes there will be short delay.

Serving police officers will always experience delays or blockages in the system. The most typical common experience is when attending a hearing at court. There's a process involved and it can be unhelpful to keep bothering the court staff or C.P.S. to try and get your case in front of others on the list. It is often preferable to accept your current circumstances, prepare yourself and wait patiently until you are called into court.

In another set of circumstances, it's not unusual to get stuck in heavy traffic and we can become frustrated and anxious. My advice is not to be aggressive but relax and even allow other drivers to go ahead of you in a line of vehicles. By doing this it will reduce the possibility of a road rage incident and the delay will usually only cost you a matter of a few seconds.

It's also important to consider that we need patience to be a good listener. If we interrupt others who are talking it is not only considered to be rude but it shows a lack of interpersonal skills. I'm sure we have all seen journalists on television trying to score a point against a politician by using this tactic by interrupting the interviewee.

Patience can also be a valuable skill when interrogating suspects as it is important not to interrupt the flow of any explanation that a suspect gives during an interview.

Developing this skill can be invaluable in a range of policing situations and can help you to keep you safe when dealing with challenging situations.

It was a few days before my retirement in 2007 when I went on foot patrol with a young Police Community officer. My retirement papers had been approved and I had already secured a new job with Tower Hamlets Council. I had completed 30 years of police service and I was entitled to claim a pension. I was 'de-mob' happy.

We patrolled Shadwell ward area that late turn without incident and as we made our way back for a refreshment break we decided to cut through the Glamis estate. This estate had experienced considerable anti-social behaviour over the years but as a result of hard work in partnership with residents it was now reasonably quiet and safe.

As we walked through the estate, I noticed a car parked in an unusual position near to the flats. It appeared to be parked in an unusual position, so I went to investigate. There was no one in the vehicle but as I approached it a man returned to the car and opened the driver's door. I had developed an instinct over the years to know that something was not quite right, so I challenged the man. He was 6 feet tall, of mixed race, in his early 20's, of athletic build and from my initial engagement I could tell he was confident and had purpose. I managed to obtain his name and address and verified ownership of the car. He was impatient and wanted to leave. I noticed out of the corner of my eye that there was a small amount of herbal cannabis in the centre consul of the car but I did not bring it to the attention of the male at this time. Instead, I asked the P.C.S.O. to call through and carry out a check on the man's name on the Police National Computer.

The response from control was hardly instant and I had to engage with the male in general conversation to keep him calm. Often, the person in the control room has no idea of what you are dealing with on the street and has little understanding of the skills that an officer has to use when stopping a suspicious person. From the delay in the response, I suspected that there may be more to this stop than possession of a small quantity of cannabis.

I was aware from the male's stature and demeanour that it would be difficult for me to subdue him if the situation became physical. However, I was prepared for physical conflict despite only having a P.C.S.O. in support.

This was not to say that I had no faith in him, as the P.C.S.O.s were very much part of the team, but I knew it would be unfair to ask him to become involved in a potentially violent arrest.

During my conversation with the male, I turned my radio down so that he would not hear the result of the name check. Nevertheless, I heard the operator nervously ask the PCSO what his location was and immediately directed another police unit to attend. I heard from the communication that the suspect was suspected of being involved in a serious sexual assault, namely rape and should be arrested for it.

I believe that the suspect must have heard the response, but I managed to divert his attention to the small amount of cannabis visible in his car. He did not seem to be too concerned about what was considered to be a relatively minor offence but I knew if I started to alert him to my intentions of detaining him for rape, he would more than likely try to escape. The ethics that were ingrained into me when I first joined the Police in Merseyside 'kicked in' and the last thing that I wanted was for him to get away.

I had handcuffs ('quick cuffs') and C.S. spray with me in case things turned nasty but I felt that I could have more control over the situation if I just kept calm, used patience together with other soft skills to minimise conflict.

Waiting for assistance in this kind of situation can be a lonely and vulnerable place especially when onlookers try to interrupt or intervene. On this occasion, a young male approached us and started to talk to the suspect. From the conversation he was having with him he appeared to know him and for a moment I could see things escalating, but at the same time a Police van screamed around the corner and stopped. Two large police officers jumped out and now the odds were on my side. When I arrested the suspect, he tried to hand over his mobile phone to the young male who approached us. I suspected that they may be incriminating evidence on his phone and we seized it. The suspect put up a bit of a struggle before being bundled into the back of the van.

We took him to Bethnal Green Police Station but unfortunately the custody office was really busy and we had to wait our turn to book the prisoner into custody. Just because I was a Sergeant it didn't give me preferential treatment to jump the queue. I had to wait in the custody office corridor with the suspect, who was complaining, insulting me, constantly asking for things but I remained calm and patient. It took nearly three hours to get him booked in and give him his rights, during which time I maintained a polite rapport with him until he was placed in a cell.

I was now able to relax, complete my arrest notes and have a well-deserved cup of tea in the sanctuary of the police canteen. It was nearly the end of my shift and we had not had anything to eat due to the arrest and delay. I knew that several hours of paperwork lay ahead of us and we would remain on duty until well into the night, but it was satisfying to know that we had successfully brought the male into custody for a serious offence with the minimum of physical force.

The de-brief

A few days after the arrest of the suspect for rape I retired from the Metropolitan Police Service.

There was no pomp or ceremony or even a handshake from a senior officer on my last afternoon. I didn't really expect special treatment on the day because after serving 30 years in the organisation you come to understand that you are merely an individual and ultimately dispensable.

This didn't mean that I did not feel a touch of sadness when I handed in my uniform and warrant card and left the rear yard of Limehouse Police Station for the final time. However, I only had a short time to reflect as I was to start another job with Tower Hamlets Council the following Monday. This would be a second career for me lasting 10 years and the opportunity enabled me to utilise my skills as I was 'head-hunted' to start a new enforcement team working closely with the Police.

Since leaving the Police, I have had an opportunity to look inwards at their work and have experienced the delivery of their service from the point of view as a member of the public and also on a couple of occasions, as a victim of crime. I have always been humble and respectful of their role and never overtly used my former position to influence them.

The service that I have received from them has varied from being excellent at one extreme to being uncaring and dismissive from the other. I continue to have respect for everyone who 'does the job' as it is usually a thankless task and people are prepared to jump all over you if you make a mistake. However, there is an increasing feeling amongst the public that the Police are distant, uncaring and not visible on the streets. This may be unfair due to the increased 'demand' from the public and accountability that the service is now under, but it may well be worth senior police officers to reflect on what used to work within the service and the simple things that can be done to improve matters.

There appears to be a concerted effort by some politicians and some areas of the media intent of criticising policing for every error of judgement. This had resulted in falling Police moral and maybe a feeling amongst rank-and-file officers that it's just not worth doing the job as no one appreciates their efforts. However, it is always right to do the job, the right way and with passion.

There have been instances for many years around malpractice, racism and wrong-doing by police officers but it must be understood that policing is a complex area and officers routinely work in a violent and chaotic environment. It is therefore unsurprising that sometimes mistakes are made.

There has also been a drive in recent years to recruit police officers who have higher academic qualifications and for probationary constables to undertake an apprenticeship where they complete a policing course to degree level. It is commendable from the point of view of attempting to raise standards but this may exclude some potential recruits who have excellent inter-personal skills but may lack an academic background.

I am in agreement with a statement recently made by Andrew Snowden, who is the Police and Crime

Commissioner of Lancashire that people with genuine 'common sense' can be effective community police officers and I would like to think that this was the category I was in when I first joined. There is certainly a requirement for personal development and continuing learning, but an officer must have genuine passion for the role and self-motivation to succeed. Without having a good, positive attitude no matter of qualifications will make the officer effective. These recruits may be officers who are content to stay in the lower ranks and want to make a difference in the communities that they serve. In fact, these officers may become **'Natural Police'**.

I will continue to 'champion' the use of 'soft' skills in the enforcement environment as they are the foundation of good policing and continue to be relevant for modern day officers. I hope that more time will be set aside in future training programmes and personal development reviews to encourage officers to learn and understand the benefits of putting these skills into practice.

Printed in Great Britain
by Amazon

12963175R00098